WEAPON

THE BARRETT RIFLE

CHRIS McNAB

Series editor Martin Pegler

MW00446176

First published in Great Britain in 2016 by Osprey Publishing, PO Box 883, Oxford, OX1 9PL, UK
PO Box 3985, New York, NY 10185-3985, USA
E-mail: info@ospreypublishing.com

Osprey Publishing, part of Bloomsbury Publishing Plc

© 2016 Osprey Publishing Ltd.

All rights reserved. Apart from any fair dealing for the purpose of private study, research, criticism or review, as permitted under the Copyright, Designs and Patents Act, 1988, no part of this publication may be reproduced, stored in a retrieval system, or transmitted in any form or by any means, electronic, electrical, chemical, mechanical, optical, photocopying, recording or otherwise, without the prior written permission of the copyright owner. Inquiries should be addressed to the Publishers.

A CIP catalog record for this book is available from the British Library

Print ISBN: 978 1 4728 1101 1
PDF ebook ISBN: 978 1 4728 1102 8
ePub ebook ISBN: 978 1 4728 1103 5

Index by Rob Munro
Typeset in Sabon and Univers
Originated by PDQ Media, Bungay, UK
Printed in China through World Print Ltd.

16 17 18 19 20   10 9 8 7 6 5 4 3 2 1

Osprey Publishing supports the Woodland Trust, the UK's leading woodland conservation charity. Between 2014 and 2018 our donations are being spent on their Centenary Woods project in the UK.

www.ospreypublishing.com

Acknowledgments
Thanks go to several people for their help with this project. A special acknowledgment goes to Jonathan Ferguson of the Royal Armouries, Leeds, for patiently taking me through the internal workings of the Barrett rifles and allowing access to weapons for photography. Thanks also go to series editor Martin Pegler, for his advice on my research, plus Osprey editor Nick Reynolds for his editorial support and illustrators Johnny Shumate and Alan Gilliland for their excellent artworks.

Editor's note
US customary measurements are used in this book. For ease of comparison please refer to the following conversion table:

1km = 0.62 miles
1m = 1.09yd / 3.28ft
1cm = 0.39in
1mm = 0.04in
1kg = 2.20lb / 35.27oz

Front-cover images: (top) Barrett M82A1 (© Royal Armouries PR.9613); (bottom) A US Army sniper takes aim with an M107 Barrett. Note the extended length of the rail on the receiver, giving complete flexibility for the mounting of optics (US Army). Title-page image: A US Marine provides security out to ranges of 1,600m (1,750yd), as fellow Marines patrol a village in Kajaki, Afghanistan, in 2010. (US DoD)

CONTENTS

INTRODUCTION

In September 2000, I had the good fortune to spend an absorbing week of research in the presence of US Marine Corps personnel in Quantico, Virginia. In addition to my diarized on-base activities and interviews, the Marines also extended a typically robust off-duty care package, part of which involved taking me to a civilian shooting range in Virginia to let fly with an assortment of firearms, weapons well beyond the legal remit of UK gun laws.

The range of firearms I handled that day was broad – M16 rifle, Glock pistol, .357 Smith & Wesson revolver, a black-powder Colt handgun (one of the smoothest weapons I have ever fired), a .30-06 hunting rifle – but all were eclipsed by what arrived in the range parking lot in the early afternoon.

From the trunk of a top-end Ferrari sports car, a gentleman who was clearly of means lifted out a Thompson submachine gun and a Barrett M82A1 rifle, and strode purposefully to the range tables. As the Barrett passed by, it elicited a knowing whistle from my Marine companion, but I was none the wiser – .50-caliber rifles are weapons that were seldom encountered in British sporting shooting circles in the early 2000s. I didn't know what was coming.

This US Marine scout sniper, conducting training in Japan in 2006, is firing a .50-caliber M82A3 Special Application Scoped Rifle (SASR), the latest iteration of the Barrett M82 line. (US DoD)

The M107 was adopted by the US Army in the 1990s and early 2000s. The lengthened accessory rail was deemed essential for the flexible positing of scopes and other tactical devices. (US DoD)

The shooting area was an enclosed space, the tables framed by a corrugated-iron housing, and just the detonations of the regular firearms were of intense volume. Then the Barrett went off. I remember my knees buckling as I adopted a semi-squat, my senses stunned by what could only be described as a sustained roar, not a swift bang. The muzzle blast sucked up dust and debris from the floor, creating a visual swirl, and the empty .50-caliber case sounded like a wind chime hitting the floor, compared to the light rounds of the other weapons. Almost everybody in the range flinched, swore, and then immediately focused their attention on the next rounds to rip out from the Barrett's muzzle. The Marine captain, an artilleryman by trade, nodded his gritty approval, telling me that the gun's report was not too dissimilar to that of a piece of field artillery.

The owner of the Barrett was also generous enough to let me shoot the gun (I think he sensed my awe), working through a full magazine. The experience was exhilarating. Although the recoil was certainly formidable, it was neither uncontrollable nor painful – the .30-06 hunting rifle I'd shot earlier in the day gave a far more shoulder-bruising punch than the Barrett. It was also accurate. Even with my rudimentary precision-shooting skills, I was getting respectable groupings, and with a bit of training probably could have done so at ranges of many hundreds of meters; and instead of raising a little dust from the gun butts, the .50 BMG rounds were blowing out fist-sized chunks of dirt.

What I was buying into was the same package of qualities that has persuaded thousands of people worldwide – military, law enforcement, and civilian – in more than 65 nations to add .50-caliber Barrett firearms to their arsenals. In summary, these qualities are: huge power and penetration, a semiautomatic action (in some models), super-long-range capabilities, reliability, user-friendliness, and accuracy.

This book is about the .50-caliber Barrett rifles, in all their forms, which I often refer to as the "Barrett" singular as a stylistic shorthand. In some ways, the story is a surprising one. The .50 BMG round, although formidable, is still incapable of punching through much of the modern vehicle armor in service today. Conversely, the same round is arguably overkill as a precision anti-personnel weapon, adding more physical

Demonstrating impressive muscle control, a US Army corporal with the 2nd Aviation Assault Battalion scans the landscape with his .50-caliber Barrett M107. Aerial sniping requires additional calculations for the aircraft's windspeed. (US Army)

destruction but little more actual kill effectiveness than, say, a .338 Lapua Magnum or 7.62mm NATO rounds, fired from guns that are generally lighter and more convenient to handle. The internet forums have the inevitable critics who claim that the .50-caliber Barrett rifle is an impractical weapon, the popularity of which is more down to its Hollywood-friendly showmanship than its genuinely practical combat applications.

Such critics are, however, quickly silenced by the legions of military personnel who have actually taken the Barrett into action and used it *in extremis*. The appreciative feedback from the battlefield is near universal. In 2005, for example, the Barrett M107 (the US Army's version of the M82A1) took first prize in the troop-nominated Top Ten inventions in the US armed services. Ronnie Barrett, the legendary figure behind the creation of the Barrett rifles, explains the significance of this award:

> We've had a lot of troops who've found great, creative ways [in which] this rifle could serve. It's just what happens when you give a good piece of equipment to a good soldier – they figure out fantastic ways of working with it. And that's what's happened with our rifle. So in 2005 we were awarded the Top Ten Invention from the US Army – never has a rifle been on that list before. It's actually asking our soldiers "What piece of equipment has enabled you to get your job done?" And we were in there with some real fantastic other pieces of equipment, like the up-armor for the Humvee, different coagulation medicines for bandages and things [like that], and here we have the Barrett M107, which has done quite well in the War against Terror. (Barrett 2008)

This award is indeed an honor and, as Mr. Barrett points out, is only given if the piece of equipment in question actually fulfills its end of the practicality bargain with the troops.

This book chronicles the technological development of the .50-caliber Barrett rifles, and their use in theaters of conflict ranging from the southern borderlands of Northern Ireland through to the jungles of South America. It will also appraise the Barrett tactically – where does it fit into the spectrum of small-arms firepower in the US armed forces, and to what roles has it been purposed? The book will also look at some of the mythologies that have grown around the Barrett. The very qualities that have led to the Barrett being lauded in real-life action have also given it a camera-ready appeal to film producers, meaning that the Barrett has cropped up in numerous movies, cast as either hero or villain. Yet unlike some weapons, which gain on-camera powers they actually don't possess in real life, the Barrett's mystique, as we shall see, is largely warranted.

DEVELOPMENT
Crafting the .50-caliber rifle

ANTECEDENTS

On September 15, 1916, during the costly Somme offensive of World War I, 36 British Mk I tanks rumbled into action at the battle of Flers–Courcelette. Their appearance on the battlefield marked the first time that tanks had been rolled out in warfare, and although this first outing had limited tactical effect on the day, its wider import was not lost on the Germans who faced them. The first instinct of the German soldiers was to open up on the angular behemoths with their rifles and machine guns, but they watched in dismay as their 7.92mm bullets simply skipped off the tanks' plate armor. Quite simply, a new weapon was required for a new target.

Thus began the long-running war between armored vehicles and anti-armor weapons, a battle that continues to this day. At first the Germans relied on good old-fashioned improvisation. A 77mm field gun, for example, could be wheeled up and fired over open sights at the lumbering tanks, the shell having no problem ripping apart the comparatively thin plate. German tank-hunting teams also became conversant in isolating the vehicles from their infantry support and then disabling them with grenade attacks through the vision slits or against the tracks. What was really needed, however, was a means for defeating the armor with stand-off accuracy.

In 1918, that means arrived in the form of the Tankgewehr M1918 ("Antitank Rifle Model 1918"), which was designed and put into production by Mauser-Werke. Essentially, it was little more than a huge, shoulder-breaking (literally so, if held incorrectly), single-shot bolt-action rifle in 13.2×92mmR caliber. It was a long and heavy contraption, hewn in wood and steel, and despite the massive kick generated by its cartridge, which launched a 795-grain steel-cored armor-piercing bullet, there were absolutely no recoil compensation features fitted. In practical terms this meant that firing just two or three rounds from this weapon would render

The massive 13.2×92mmR bullet from a German Tankgewehr M1918 of World War I, sitting next to a British .303in Lee-Enfield round. Following the capture of Tankgewehr rifles and ammunition in 1918, the 13mm round provided the Americans with the inspiration to develop the .50 BMG cartridge. (Author's collection)

the operator bruised and breathless. Nevertheless, the M1918 worked: its round punched through 0.59in of armor at 300m (328yd), enough to penetrate inside the British tanks.

Predictably enough, armor itself increased in thickness during the interwar years and became more sophisticated in composition. In response, purpose-designed antitank artillery guns emerged, and their explosive high-velocity shells did a far more convincing job of dispatching a tank than the single bullet from an antitank rifle. Yet the antitank rifle persisted, partly on account of its convenience (it required a single operator rather than a gun team with all its accompanying logistics) and partly because there were other targets on the battlefield. By the time World War II broke out in September 1939, the military mechanization that had begun in the previous conflict had reached flourishing vitality. Antitank rifles suddenly had a broader range of target opportunities – trucks, armored cars, self-propelled guns, half-tracks, aircraft (on the ground), and anything else beyond the destructive capabilities of regular small-arms ammunition.

The principal manufacturers of antitank rifles in World War II were Britain, Poland, and the Soviet Union. The British produced the infamous .55 Boys antitank rifle, which could penetrate 0.74in of homogenous armor angled at 90 degrees at 460m (503yd), and the Poles gave German armored vehicle crews genuine concern with their 7.92×107mm DS Wz. 35. Both of these weapons were bolt-action, magazine-fed types, but the Soviets took a technological step forward with the gas-operated, semiautomatic PTRS-41, chambered for a mighty 14.5×114mm round. A single-shot bolt-action rifle, the PTRD, fired the same cartridge from a cheaper system.

The rationale behind antitank rifles remained credible, just, for many nations at the beginning of World War II, when tank armor was still relatively thin. But the strength of armor relentlessly increased during the war, not only in main battle tanks but also in other varieties of infantry combat vehicle (ICV). Thus by around 1943, antitank rifles were actually fairly impotent against modern main battle tanks and many other armored vehicles. Furthermore, the advent of man-portable shaped-charge rocket weapons, such as the bazooka and *Panzerfaust*, meant that there were far better options available for destroying enemy armored vehicles.

The Soviets did use such guns as sniper weapons on the Eastern Front in 1943–45, but the antitank rifle effectively died out altogether in the first decades of the Cold War. Even so, the idea of a rifle capable of performing heavier destructive purpose than killing humans lingered on ...

ANTI-MATERIEL RIFLES AND THE BARRETT M82A1

As the Cold War stirred into life, producing wars of varying magnitude around the world, it slowly but steadily became apparent that there was something of a gap in the small-arms arsenals of professional armies. Precision firepower was in the hands of the snipers, equipped with purpose-designed bolt-action or semiautomatic rifles of medium calibers such as 7.62mm, .308, and .338. Firing accurized ammunition, and handled by steady shots using good scopes, these rifles were capable of hitting and taking down human targets out to ranges of 1,000m (1,093yd), although 600m (656yd) was a more realistic boundary.

In the US forces, one interesting diversion from the use of precision sniper rifles related to improvisations with the .50 BMG Browning M2HB machine gun. At its heart, the M2HB was, and remains, an immensely destructive area weapon, capable of raining down a shattering stream of .50-caliber rounds out to 2,000m (2,187yd) and beyond. Note, however, that the M2HB can also be set to fire single rounds if required, usually for ranging, but sometimes applied consciously to other purposes. In both the Korean War (1950–53) and the Vietnam War (1963–75), there were instances in which US troops clamped telescopic sights to .50-caliber machine guns and, using the guns in the single-shot mode, engaged point targets way beyond the reach of many other sniper weapons. The legendary Vietnam War sniper Carlos Hathcock even claimed a Viet Cong (VC) opponent in this manner at a range of 2,500yd. An additional bonus of the .50-caliber as a sniper cartridge was that its kinetic force was capable of smashing a vehicle engine or other large pieces of military equipment, destroying them for the few dollars' cost of a bullet, rather than the thousands of dollars required for an airdropped bomb or missile, or an antitank launcher. Although these early innovators wouldn't have known it, they were laying the foundations for the long-range anti-materiel rifle. Yet actually designing a rifle for the .50-caliber was not

The Barrett M82 in its early days, photographed in 1986. Note, in contrast to the later M82A1, the non-vented lower receiver and the flat-type muzzle brake. (US DoD)

seriously considered, the cartridge considered simply too potent for a shoulder-mounted weapon. Ronnie Barrett thought otherwise.

Born in 1954 in Murfreesboro, Tennessee, Ronnie Barrett is today one of the true legends in firearms design, an individual who broke the mold of conventional thought and has given the world a unique and influential series of firearms. In the early 1980s, the young Ronnie Barrett was actually working as a photographer, but was a keen enthusiast in the arts of sport shooting and weapon design. With the impetuousness of youth on his side, he spotted a potential gap in the market. Here Ronnie himself takes over the narrative:

Like most gun people I was born interested in guns and firearms. I started out with a little BB gun and .22s, then I got into adult firearms – I think the first firearm that I purchased was a .45 pistol and I carried that ever since I was legally able and I haven't put it down yet. But then you get into competitions, from handguns to machine guns to high-powered rifles, and in this sport you keep wanting the next best firearm and the most powerful firearm … so I wanted a .50-caliber. Of course there was no commercially available .50-caliber rifle, so you ended up just having to make your own. As I was not a great admirer of slow bolt-action rifles, I wanted a semi-automatic, so at the age of 28 I decided that I would make one myself. In my youthful years it was one of those things where I didn't think I couldn't do it, so I just got out there and did it. I had no experience in manufacturing and engineering; I was actually a photographer, a job that I had back in high school. My photography studio down town had a short [shooting] range with a little bullet trap at the end of it, so at nighttime we would close down the photography studio and me and a few other fellow police officers would come down and fire the handguns down the hallway. We would sweep it [shell casings] up before next morning's business.

Anyway, on photographing a boat for the Rainbow company in December one day in 1982 – this was a gunboat made by the Rainbow company in Nashville who make the .50-caliber Browning machine guns – I really got interested in that .50-cal. I decided that, well, I was talking to [a Rainbow representative] and said "You know, if I went back and designed a .50-cal rifle, would you guys be interested in making it?" So what does a grown man tell a 28-year-old kid – "We can do that." I took it seriously and went back and started sketching out things in three dimensions, as an artist would, and after a couple of months I had a design, based on a recoil-operated, recoiling barrel, .50-cal design. I've got this rifle here in the R&D department – it's heavy and it looks like something that came in from the Civil War. But anyway, the gun worked and we found a one-bay garage with a machine shop that would put up with me, and then worked in the evening hours from 5 o'clock to 12 o'clock at night, and four months later we had a little gun that was shooting, kinda shooting. It told me everything I needed to know to correct to go to generation 2, so we started the gen no. 2 and went back to the Rainbow company to show them my gun. Things didn't work out, so I decided to take out an ad

in *Shotgun News* and go to the Houston Gun Show and carry it here and carry it there; and after a while I had people who were saying "Hey, if you make another one, I'd like one of those." So with a little help from the bank I made a batch of 30 rifles, which was quite difficult to do ... (Barrett 2008)

A Barrett M82 used in the Gulf War of 1990–91. The early cylindrical muzzle brake immediately jumps out as being different from the standardized arrowhead-shaped brake. (US DoD)

The gun that Ronnie had created was the M82 Light-Fifty, a .50-caliber semiautomatic monster that commanded attention. Ronnie explained that making the guns was one thing, but pricing them correctly was quite another, and there was much financial trial and error before the guns began to turn a profit; but, having delivered the first batch of 30 rifles, he then produced and sold another 30, and the Barrett enterprise began to flourish.

The gun that truly fueled this growth was the now-famous Barrett **M82A1**, introduced in 1986 as the principal version of the original M82 model. Just a quick glance at the M82A1 told potential users that something different was going on here. First, the weapon was seriously big – an overall length of 75in (with a 29in barrel) and weighing in empty at 32.72lb – thus necessitating the folding bipod set beneath the front receiver. Everything about the gun spoke of solidity; from the massive barrel terminating in the arrowhead-shaped muzzle brake through to the beefy two-part receiver and ten-round magazine. Atop the receiver was a long steel rail for scope mounting.

Apart from its physical dimensions, the M82A1 offered other features that instantly grabbed press and military attention. First was the cartridge. The properties of the .50 BMG are examined in depth in the next chapter, but suffice to say here that the M82A1 could deliver a bullet at greater range and with more destructive force on target than any other tactical or hunting

THE BARRETT RIFLE EXPOSED

.50 BMG Barrett M82A1 rifle

1. Upper receiver	**10.** Barrel spring assembly	**19.** Bolt carrier
2. Main spring	**11.** Bipod	**20.** Cocking lever
3. Rear ladder sight	**12.** Magazine	**21.** Bolt
4. Telescopic sight	**13.** Trigger guard	**22.** Firing pin
5. Barrett Optical Sighting System	**14.** Trigger	**23.** Round in chamber
6. Carrying handle (folded down)	**15.** Pistol grip	**24.** Firing-pin extension spring
7. Scope base	**16.** Rear hand grip	**25.** Magazine-release catch
8. Fluted barrel	**17.** Recoil pad	**26.** Firing-pin extension
9. Muzzle brake	**18.** Sear	**27.** Transfer bar assembly

M82A1 specifications

Caliber: .50 BMG or .416 Barrett

Operation: Semiautomatic

Weight: 32.72lb or 31.45lb

Overall length: 57in or 48in

Barrel length: 29in or 20in (.50 BMG only)

Barrel twist rate: 1 turn in 15in (.50 BMG) or 1 turn in 12in (.416 Barrett)

Rail length/MOA: 18in/27 MOA

Magazine capacity: Ten rounds

rifle available. More than that, the M82A1 managed to contain the power of the cartridge within a semiautomatic, short-recoil mechanism, fed from a ten-shot magazine. The semiautomatic configuration was a bold choice. Traditionally, bolt-action rifles are held as the best tools for delivering long-range shots, as they seat the cartridge with minimal damage to the bullet and maximum feed consistency. The mechanical cycling of a semiautomatic mechanism is far harder on the round, however, and can impart damage to a bullet that can make a significant ballistic difference over hundreds of yards of flight. Such is the theory, but in reality well-engineered semiautomatic mechanisms such as that built into the Barrett can seat rounds smoothly and dependably, without a truly critical effect on overall accuracy. Furthermore, the semiautomatic mechanism provided that most-valued of attributes for a sniper – a quick follow-up shot, ideal for breaking down tough-material objects or switching between dispersed targets.

The M82A1 began to take off commercially with the heavy-caliber civilian shooting fraternity in the United States, but as Ronnie Barrett noted, it wasn't long before the military began to take notice:

It began to work, and then I started to attract some military applications for it. This is something that the anti-gunners have gotten into, that this was a gun designed for the military that has fallen into the hands of civilians. It wasn't that way at all. It was a gun for sportsmen, made for my hobby, and sold to sportsmen, paid for out of sportsmen's pockets and the military found an application for it. And actually, our government and 50 other governments found the benefit of the relationship between the civilian and the government industries, where again the government is able to use something that the civilian has invented. Many of our guns and much of our equipment has found its way into government service.

So anyway, around 1989 we had a foreign government, Sweden actually, that was interested in 100 guns, and we built those and sold those. And when *Desert Storm* broke out

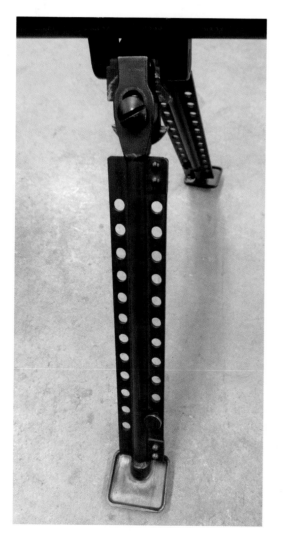

The bipod of the M82A1 has flat feet to allow it to sit comfortably on hard surfaces, although spiked-feet options are available. (Author's photo, © Royal Armouries PR.12187)

there was enough of our guns in the hands of the US military – one here, two there, that they had been working with and training on … and so when *Desert Storm* broke out our troops knew what to do. And so they started placing orders for them and emergency orders to go to the front. The Marine Corps officially adopted it then; the US Army was a little skeptical, so over the next ten or so years the US Army did tests on my gun and on [the guns] of anybody else who could submit for a competitive trial. And so after a lot of competition they selected the best gun, and the Barrett M82A1 became adopted as the M107. So having the big army as a customer was very nice; they gave us a very substantial order and they entrenched the Barrett rifle into history now and forever … (Barrett 2008)

This view of the M82A1's side receiver shows the short scope-mounting block atop the receiver; later models received full-length Picatinny rails. (Author's photo, © Royal Armouries PR.12187)

The defining arrowhead muzzle brake of the Barrett M82A1, the photo clearly showing the rearward path of the muzzle blast deflection. (Author's photo, © Royal Armouries PR.12187)

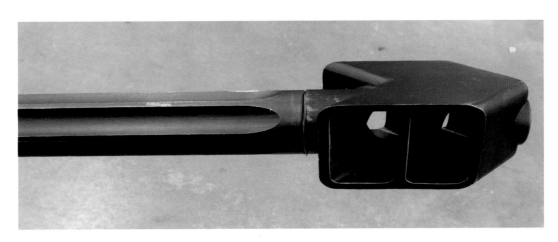

AN EVOLVING RANGE

As Ronnie concludes in this passage, it was the Barrett's shift into the military market that really cemented the .50-caliber rifle's place in commercial and tactical history. Yet the adoption of the M107 requires a little analysis to show how the Barrett range of weapons was also beginning to evolve and expand. In August 1996, the US Army, its interest pricked by the US Marine Corps' new love affair with the M82A1, publicized its desire to acquire a Caliber .50 Sniper Rifle (CFSR) system for its infantry forces. Contractors who wanted to enter this competitive bid had to present a .50-caliber weapon that was reliable, powerful, capable of landing shots out to 1,500–2,000m (1,640–2,187yd), and which weighed less than 30lb (ideally 25lb with a loaded five-round magazine). Total length had to be less than 40in, with 36in being the objective. The gun's accuracy had to be equal to its power. It required a MIL-STD-1913 Picatinny-type rail for scope mounting, with a repeat zero within a ½ minute of angle (MOA) when the scope was removed and remounted.

Barrett Firearms Manufacturing, Inc. was naturally well placed to enter this competition, but the M82A1 was not the first gun it presented. (It should be noted that by this time Barrett was also not the only company to be producing .50-caliber rifles; Barrett's competitors will be discussed further later in this book.) Back in 1987, Barrett Firearms Manufacturing, Inc. introduced a variation of the M82A1 into its catalogue. This was the **M82A2**, another .50-caliber semiautomatic rifle, but this time reworked into a bullpup configuration, with the magazine set behind the trigger group. By laying out the gun in this way, the overall length dropped slightly to 55.5in, although barrel length remained the same. Unlike its immediate forebears, the M82A2 was mounted with the shoulder pressed into a special curved rest set just behind the magazine well, the rear of the receiver running across the top of the shoulder to give the weapon an appearance akin to a shoulder-mounted rocket launcher. To give the operator further stability, a vertical grip was provided underneath the front of the receiver. The scope mount was also moved forward to allow for the new layout. Performance data was roughly the same as that of the M82A1.

The M82A2 was an interesting concept, but one that did not catch on with the military community or civilian buyers, and it was relatively quickly discontinued. The bullpup layout, however, lived on in two other designs. The first was the **M90**, produced between 1990 and 1995.

The M82A2 was one Barrett product line that didn't really take off, largely on account of its unusual mounting system. The curved rest set just behind the magazine well made the primary contact with the shoulder. (Tomketchum)

The bolt-action M95 has a unitized buttplate, magazine well, and trigger housing, to improve the strength of the steel lower receiver. (Author's photo, © Royal Armouries XII.11067)

Essentially, the M90 was a bolt-action equivalent of the M82A2, the semiautomatic action of the M82A1 being replaced by a hefty manual bolt with three large lugs turning and locking directly into the barrel extension. Instead of the ten-round detachable box magazine of the M82A1, the M90 sported a shorter five-round magazine.

The M90 was produced between 1990 and 1995, when it was superseded by an improved version, the **M95**. The improvements that distinguished the M95 from the M90 were evolutionary rather than transformative. The distance between the trigger group and the magazine well was increased by 1in, to improve the gun's handling. The angle of the bolt action was also canted backward to facilitate an easier loading grip; on the M90, the handle was in the direct vertical position. There were also some internal improvements to the trigger and firing-pin

An M107 used by the US Army's 10th Mountain Division in Afghanistan. The Barrett weapon has proved itself able to cope with sand ingress, partly because the power of the system pulverizes sand particles. (US DoD)

M95 specifications

Caliber: .50 BMG

Operation: Bolt-action repeater

Weight: 23.5lb

Overall length: 45in

Barrel length/type: 29in fluted

Barrel twist rate: 1 turn in 15in

Rail length/MOA: 11.75in/27 MOA

Magazine capacity: Five rounds

M107A1 specifications

Caliber: .50 BMG

Operation: Semiautomatic, recoil-operated

Weight: 28.7lb or 27.4lb

Overall length: 57in or 48in

Barrel length: 29in or 20in

Barrel twist rate: 1 turn in 15in

Rail length/MOA: 18in/27 MOA

Magazine capacity: Ten rounds

mechanisms; and also to the barrel chamber, chromium lining of which provided a smoother surface for improved feed and extraction.

The M90 and M95 both appealed to civilian, law-enforcement, and military personnel. An M95, for example, was not only an impressive 12in shorter than the M82A1 (overall length was 45in), it was also dramatically lighter (23.5lb) because it did not have the extra weight of the M82A1's recoiling barrel assembly – yet it still packed the same wallop of the .50-caliber round. At least 15 countries around the world adopted the M95 into their arsenals, and it was also the gun that was submitted to the US Army's CFSR competition.

Against a range of competitors, the M95 won the day and Barrett was awarded the contract, the gun being redesignated XM107 for US Army use. After the contract had been awarded, however, it became apparent to the US ordnance authorities that a semiautomatic design was actually far more tactically compelling, so the competition seemed to open up once again. Barrett had an advantage, however, in that it had been upgrading the M82A1 along the way. The **M82A1A**, for example, was an enhanced M82A1 better able to handle the new precision .50-caliber Mk 211 Mod 0 explosive round. A more significant step forward was the **M82A1M**. This gun had a rear under-stock hand grip plus a monopod fitting beneath the butt, to configure the firing position with custom precision. Running along the top of the gun was an extended Picatinny rail. The M82A1M also had back-up iron sights fitted, in case of loss of or damage to the scope, and featured a removable carrying handle.

The M82A1M was adopted by the US military in two official forms. The US Marines took it on board as the M82A3 SASR (Special Applications Scoped Rifle), minus the rear monopod, while the US Army eventually accepted it in the role of the CFSR, officially adopted as the XM107 LRSR (Long Range Sniper Rifle) in October 2001. The wheels of approval turned steadily, with the weapon type being designated as the **M107** in 2003 and given "full material release" (open distribution to the troops) in 2005.

CONTINUAL ENHANCEMENTS

Barrett has never been a company to stand still, and since 2005 the M107 has been the recipient of a variety of modifications and upgrades. Recognizing that the Barrett's dimensions limited its use in confined environments such as ships, helicopters, and from inside armored vehicles, Barrett issued the **M107CQ**, which is 9in shorter and 5lb lighter than the standard rifle. In 2010, Barrett also launched a significant upgrade to the design in the form of the **M107A1**. The dimensions and performance of the new gun were largely the same as those of the M107, but through material innovations the M107A1 had, like the M107CQ, shed 5lb in weight. More obviously, the gun is designed to take Barrett's QDL quick-attach suppressor, hence the Barrett's traditional arrowhead muzzle brake has been replaced by a four-port cylindrical design. The bolt-carrier group has also been through a redesign, to ensure that the semiautomatic action continues to function reliably even with the different recoil characteristics imparted by the suppressor. The official Barrett publicity explains that the bolt group has received "a mix of ultra-hard coatings and advanced nickel Teflon® plating that increases lubricity, is corrosion-resistant and greatly eases cleaning."

The M82A1CQ was developed with more compact dimensions to facilitate its use in confined environments. Note the full-length rail, cylindrical muzzle brake, and flipped-up iron sights. (Author's photo, © Royal Armouries B.0847 1)

Material advances abound in the M107A1. A thermal cheek piece on the stock protects the user's cheek against heat or cold injuries in extreme environments. Both bore and chamber are fully chrome lined, and the modified aluminum rear grip is rail mounted for easy user-specific configuration. The magazine is given witness holes, so the shooter can tell at a glance how many rounds of ammunition he has left in the magazine.

In 2006, Barrett Firearms Manufacturing, Inc. also unveiled a new semiautomatic .50 BMG, the **XM500**. Details about this weapon are somewhat scarce, and it is not listed in the current product range on the company's website. The core difference appears to be that the XM500 is gas rather than recoil operated, with a fixed barrel and a bullpup layout to reduce the overall dimensions of the gun. According to some sources, the XM500 is still in development, so it is one to watch for the future.

Also in development, and even more radical in nature, is the **XM109 AMPR** (Anti-Materiel Payload Rifle). Designed to defeat armored vehicles, and other substantial materiel targets, out to 2,000m (2,187yd) range, the XM109 fires a 25×59mm round, which offers both impact and airburst capabilities. The gun itself has the lower receiver of the M107, but a new

The XM109 fires no less than a 25mm cartridge, delivering explosive effects out to more than 2,000m (2,187yd). The visibly short barrel means that recoil management is one of the greatest challenges to getting the weapon to production. (US DoD)

19

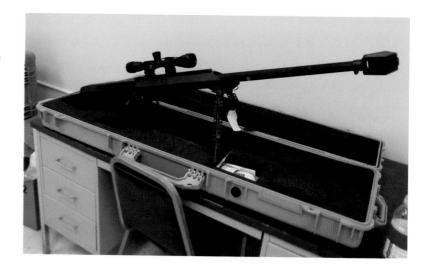

The Barrett M99 is a precision bolt-action firearm available in .50 BMG or .416 Barrett. The barrel fluting serves to keep the weapon's weight down to manageable levels. (Karl Bitz)

upper receiver; overall length is 46in, barrel length 17.6in, and total weight 33lb. Looking at the available literature, a key objective of the XM109 development program is to reduce the gun's formidable recoil, but such weapons are likely to become familiar additions to, and expansions of, US military firepower over the coming years.

Returning to the "smaller" calibers, capping off Barrett's current .50-caliber range is the **M99**. Although modern semiautomatic sniper rifles deliver excellent levels of long-range accuracy, there is little argument that the finest grades of accuracy come from bolt-action rifles. This accuracy has its ultimate expression in the M99, a single-shot bolt-action rifle available in both .50 BMG and .416 Barrett (note that the M82A1 is also available in .416 Barrett). The integrity of the bolt is at the heart of such a weapon; the M99's single-piece bolt has no fewer than 15 lugs to lock it hard and fast into the barrel extension. There are other material refinements. Most Barretts have a two-piece pressed-steel receiver, but the M99 has instead a single-piece aluminum-alloy receiver, enhancing the gun's structural strength while reducing the weight. Barrel options are a match-grade 29in fluted version or a heavy 32in version, the rifling twist differing between the calibers available. Total weight for the gun is 25lb or 23lb, depending on the barrel choice. Scopes are mounted on an M1913 steel optics rail, set on the top of the receiver parallel with the bore.

The M99 is an exceptional competition gun or (depending on the preference of the user for magazine-fed weapons) law-enforcement weapon. Yet while the M99 is the last (to date) of the .50-caliber weapons, it should be noted that Barrett's range of firearms is not purely consigned to big-caliber weapons. The company makes some other sniper weapons in non-.50-calibers, such as the bolt-action **M98B**, a ten-round repeater

M99 specifications

Caliber: .50 BMG or .416 Barrett

Operation: Single-shot bolt-action

Weight: 25lb or 23lb

Overall length: 50in or 47in

Barrel length: 32in heavy (both calibers) or 29in fluted (.50 BMG only)

Barrel twist rate: 1 turn in 15in (.50 BMG) or 1 turn in 12in (.416 Barrett)

Rail length/MOA: 13.75in/27 MOA

Magazine capacity: Single-shot

available in .338 Lapua Magnum, .300 Winchester Magnum, .308 Winchester, and 7mm Remington Magnum, with barrel-length options ranging from 16in up to 24in.

An alternative purchase of note is the **MRAD** (Multi-Role Adaptive Design), another bolt-action weapon developed for US Special Operations Command following their launch in 2009 of a competition for a Precision Sniper Rifle. Although Barrett did not win that bid – it was taken in 2013 by the Remington MSR (Modular Sniper Rifle) – the MRAD remains a sophisticated and persuasive piece of kit. It is bolt action, fed from a ten-round magazine. Ergonomics and modularity are the keywords with the MRAD. The stock – which is hinged and can be folded flat alongside the receiver – is fully adjustable for both cheek weld and length of pull. To give the rifle true modularity, the MRAD can change calibers by swapping barrels; the barrel change is performed from the front of the gun by loosening two bolts with a Torz wrench. Available calibers are .338 Lapua Magnum, .300 Winchester Magnum, .308 Winchester, .260 Remington, and 6.5mm Creedmoor.

Before moving on to an analysis of .50-caliber Barrett rifles in action, one final weapon in the Barrett range deserves a mention – the **REC7**. Unlike the other guns in the Barrett series, the REC7 represents a deviation into the ultra-competitive landscape of assault rifles. (Actually, the REC7 is not the company's first foray into automatic weapons – that came with the Barrett M468, a variant of the M4 carbine but chambered for the heavier 6.8 SPC round.) The more modern REC7, released in 2007, moved away from the direct-impingement gas system of the M468 to embrace a short-stroke gas piston. It is available in the familiar 5.56mm NATO, but also the heavier 6.8 SPC, a caliber that is garnering much debate as a possible replacement for the smaller NATO round. The Unique Selling Point of the REC7 is explained by the expansion of its name – Reliability-Enhanced Carbine. Every aspect of the build of the REC7 places an emphasis on battle-hardened durability, while the free-floating, hammer-forged barrel gives a point-shooting capability at more than 600m (656yd).

The REC7 will likely sell well to specialist civilian, law-enforcement, and special-forces units. With the future of the M4 carbine in the US armed services still up for discussion, the REC7 could possibly play a larger part in the future replacement of that seminal weapon.

The Barrett series of weapons reveals a company that has innovated intensively around the theme of delivering heavy, long-range precision firepower in either bolt-action or semiautomatic formats. Of course, designing a weapon is one thing; using it in action is quite another.

The bolt-action MRAD is a fully modular rifle, being adaptable to the shooter's preferences both in terms of the caliber and the gun's ergonomics. (Barrett Firearms Manufacturing, Inc.)

USE
Long-range devastation

A NEW BATTLEFIELD ENVIRONMENT

In January 1991, Operation *Desert Storm* was unleashed in the Middle East against Saddam Hussein's Iraqi forces. In what was a landmark operation in military history, a US-led coalition utterly routed the opposition at all tactical and operational levels, from small-unit infantry actions through to predatory round-the-clock attacks by an awesome array of coalition aircraft.

Despite the conclusive and swift nature of the victory, however, Operation *Desert Storm* yielded a salutary spectrum of lessons for modern Western and Middle Eastern armies. One of these lessons, still being learned today in war zones such as Afghanistan, was the issue of small-arms range. In the 1991 US tables of organization and equipment (TO&E), the M16A2 was the standard-issue rifle; it had a theoretical point-target range of up to 600m (656yd), although in reality the effective range of engagement was about half that distance. For anything more distant, there were two main options: machine guns for area targets, and sniper rifles for point targets.

The main sniper rifle of the US Marine Corps at that time was the 7.62×51mm M40A1, essentially a military classified version of the Remington 700. The M40A1 is a fine bolt-action rifle – robust, super-accurate thanks to its 24in heavy match-grade barrel, comfortable to use, and stabilized on a bipod mounted at the front of the forend. More recent versions of the M40 are still in use, and the US Army also uses a long-action version of the Remington 700, the M24 SWS (Sniper Weapon System). So why did the Marine Corps place a rush order for a batch of 120 Barrett rifles at the outset of the Gulf War conflict?

Operation *Desert Storm* was not the first time the Marines had taken the Barrett into operations. During the 1980s, in both Beirut and Panama,

the USMC had deployed small numbers of the .50-caliber rifles to test and evaluate their utility and relevance in modern warfare. These early experiments bore fruit. In Panama, for instance, the guns were used to disable General Manuel Noriega's Panamanian Defense Forces combat aircraft before they could even take flight, the multi-million-dollar aircraft looking forlorn with wrecked engines, cockpits, and flight surfaces.

So the Marines had an informed inkling that the Barrett would be useful in the war against Saddam Hussein, for two main reasons: range and power. In the matter of range, the M40A1 and its successors are generally regarded as accurate weapons over a maximum of 914m (1,000yd). Such reach is useful and practical, but operational conditions in *Desert Storm* were a little different. Prior to 1991, much of Western military training was designed for European temperate zones, in which the undulations of countryside and the presence of trees and other natural obstacles generally limit distant visibility. Furthermore, the last major conflict the US forces had fought was the Vietnam War, in which combat ranges in the tropical hinterland might be a matter of just a few yards. Now the Western coalition was fighting in desert and arid equatorial landscapes – the first time it had done so to any notable degree since 1943 – and here the landscape was often pool-table flat, with visibility measured in kilometers and not meters.

In such a setting, targets of opportunity might be tantalizingly out of reach for an M40, but those same targets would have to be very distant indeed to escape the long arm of a Barrett rifle. By way of example, the longest confirmed sniper kill of the Gulf War conflict was achieved by a Barrett-armed Marine, who killed his target at a range of no less than 1,800m (1,968yd). That distance has since been surpassed – and substantially so – by the Barrett and a host of other rifles. One Marine sniper who fought in *Desert Storm*, Corporal Greg A. Gradwohl, explained the importance of the Barrett rifle during the conflict: "During most of the

Three US Marines, one of them providing security with his Barrett M82A1, conduct a training exercise from the roof of the American Embassy on Oahu, Hawaii in 1996. (US DoD)

A sniper with the 22nd Marine Expeditionary Unit (Special Operations Capable)'s Maritime Special Purpose Force (MSPF) ejects a 7.62mm cartridge case from his M40A1 sniper rifle during a live-fire training exercise, 2005. (US DoD)

conflict, our usual .30-caliber M-40 was next to worthless due to the extreme range and lack of cover available. Without the M82A1, my sniper team would not have been nearly as effective as we were during that conflict" (quoted in Lewis 2011: 109). In plain terms, if a unit is equipped with a Barrett rifle its zone of lethality is dramatically expanded – a practical outcome that was of huge advantage to the forces operating in the deserts of Kuwait and Iraq.

When it comes to addressing the matter of terminal ballistics, it is important to note that although the Barrett has attracted most press for its dramatic anti-personnel shots, the weapon is fundamentally an anti-materiel rifle (AMR). An AMR has to carry the sheer kinetic energy and bullet weight to smash up most heavy equipment; and in Operation *Desert Storm*, US Marines armed with Barretts had a field day. Radar dishes, radio antennae and broadcasting devices, generators and transformers, trucks and soft-skinned vehicles, light armored vehicles, missile systems, field kitchens, ammunition supplies, fuel tanks, machine guns, various types of artillery, and boxes of supplies – there was a near-endless selection

Two US soldiers begin the process of assembling a Barrett M107. The scope would need re-zeroing for long-range shots after assembly. (US DoD)

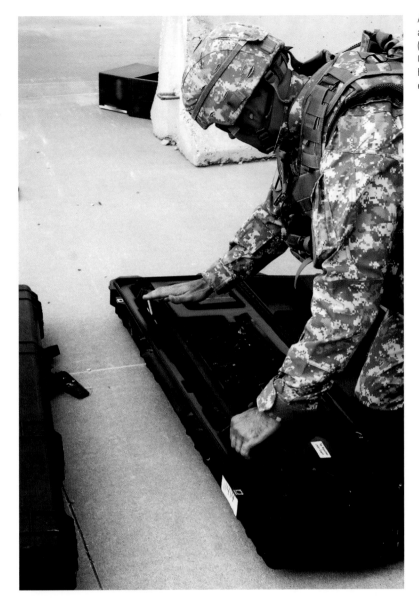

A Barrett rifle is packed away by an explosives ordnance disposal (EOD) specialist of the 641st Ordnance Company, Task Force Falcon, following a training exercise in 2008. (US DoD)

of targets that could be chewed up and disabled by the .50-caliber round at distance. In fact, such is the efficacy of the cartridge that an article in *Jane's International Defence Review* declared that "from an operational standpoint, the closest parallel weapon to a 0.50-calibre rifle is probably the 60mm mortar" (Jane's 1994: 67). Just think about that from a cost-effectiveness point of view. The author is not privy to the amount the US armed services pay for individual items of ammunition, but a reputable British source puts the cost of individual 60mm shells at £185–£640, depending on their sophistication. A quick check of the internet showed a private seller clearing out 13 rounds of .50-caliber Mk 211 Raufoss armor-piercing incendiary rounds – the most expensive and impressive of the Barrett-compatible cartridges – for $40. On that basis, the Barrett is as much a cost-cutting option as a force expander.

OPERATING THE BARRETT

Before going on to explore some of the practical and tactical issues of using the Barrett, a fundamental understanding of what is going on mechanically when a Barrett is fired is required. Here we will look specifically at the operating cycle of the M107/M82A1, as this is the weapon which attracts the lion's share of focus in this book.

Loading and firing

The first stage is, of course, to load the rifle. Cartridges are loaded into the magazine by pressing them down onto the spring-loaded platform between the feed lips, maintaining the pressure until each cartridge snaps under the lips. Although the stated capacity of the M107 is ten rounds, the official manual advice is that the user should only load a maximum of eight or nine rounds, to prevent weakening of the magazine spring.

Once the magazine is charged, it is then inserted into the magazine well, the user first connecting the magazine hook onto the hinge at the front of the magazine well, then clicking the magazine up and back to connect with the rear magazine catch. At this point the gun is still inert, with the safety on and no round in the chamber. To load the first round, the charging handle on the bolt is lifted up, pulled to the rear, then released under the power of the main spring to strip a cartridge from the top of the magazine and guide it into the chamber. As the bolt enters the barrel extension, several mechanical events occur. A bolt-latch trip, located on the inside of the upper receiver, activates the bolt-trip mechanism, which allows the bolt to retract into the bolt carrier. To achieve the very solid locking required to handle the .50-caliber round, a cam-and-pin arrangement rotates the bolt head to lock the head's three substantial locking lugs into the barrel extension. As the bolt closes up, an extractor claw also engages with the rim of the cartridge.

The gun is now loaded, and the operator can now flick the gun's selector to the "fire" position and take the first shot. Pulling the trigger results in the transfer bar pushing against the sear, which in turn is pushed

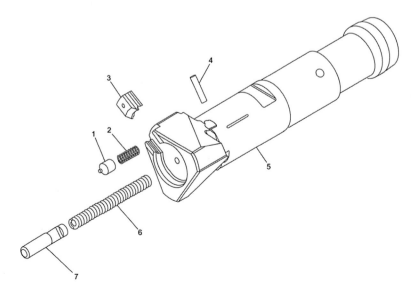

The M107 bolt assembly: (**1**) extractor; (**2**) extractor spring; (**3**) extractor claw; (**4**) ejector pin; (**5**) bolt; (**6**) ejector spring; (**7**) ejector. (US Army)

The Barrett magazine, with .50-caliber rounds loaded. At the front of the magazine can be seen the hook that engages with the front edge of the magazine well. (US DoD)

up and eventually, at the trigger's firing point, disconnects with the firing-pin extension, releasing the firing pin under spring pressure to strike the primer of the cartridge and begin the detonation sequence. The gun now fires, and as the bullet travels down the bore and out of the muzzle, huge recoil forces are imparted on the bolt face via the cartridge head. The bolt carrier, bolt, and barrel – still firmly locked together through the engagement of barrel lugs with the barrel extension – recoil for a short distance before they are unlocked as a cam groove in the bolt surface engages with a fixed pin to rotate the bolt out of engagement. Furthermore, an accelerator device strikes a shoulder around the trigger group and pivots, in turn driving an accelerator rod (which runs through and protrudes from the front of the bolt carrier) against the barrel extension, providing a further "kick" to ensure that the bolt travels vigorously backward through a full recoil cycle. Once disconnected from the bolt, the barrel returns to its original position via the impulse of two barrel springs which connect the barrel with the upper receiver.

As the bolt group continues its rearward journey, the extractor claw draws the empty cartridge case from the chamber; then a spring-powered ejector running through the bolt head snaps outward, flipping the spent case out through the ejection port on the side of the gun. To ready the gun during the recoil cycle, a cocking lever pushes the transfer bar to disengage it from the trigger, the transfer bar being held down by the disconnector until the user releases the pressure on the trigger and allows the trigger to reset. The cocking lever swings on a pin during the rearward movement, and in so doing draws back the firing pin, compressing the firing-pin extension spring; the sear catches up the firing-pin extension, holding it to the rear in preparation for the next shot.

Once the energy of the recoil is overcome by the force built up in the main return spring, the bolt group returns at speed to the front, performing the actions of loading and locking as explained at the beginning of this sequence.

A close-up shot of the M82A1's bolt group sitting in the lower receiver. The bolt head is engaged in the barrel extension and the accelerator rod can be seen pressing against the rear of the extension. (Author's photo, © Royal Armouries PR.12187)

Cleaning and maintenance

Complex to describe, but cycling in milliseconds, the Barrett's operating system is actually extremely robust, despite the violent nature of its cycle. Like all firearms, however, the Barrett needs regular care and attention to keep it working properly. Allowing dirt to build up in the moving parts, or lubricating the weapon improperly, can lead to a range of malfunctions, including failure to feed and chamber cartridges, problems with bolt locking, failure to fire (the consequence of an obstructed or retarded firing pin), failure to extract, and – if stubborn dirt is allowed to build up in the muzzle brake – excessively hard recoil.

For troops in the field, any weapon that is a challenge to disassemble is not going to endear itself; and one of the reasons why the Barrett has become entrenched in global military service is that it is simplicity itself to strip down to its basic component parts. In essence, the M82A1/M107 sits in three major component assemblies (the assemblies in which the gun is presented when first delivered to the customer). First there is the stamped-steel upper receiver, which holds the barrel and its recoil springs plus the optics rail. This marries up with the lower receiver, consisting of the stock, mainspring and buffer, trigger group, and lower frame with attached bipod. Sandwiched between these two assemblies is the bolt-carrier group. Dividing the upper receiver from the lower receiver, and thereby extracting the bolt group, is a simple matter of removing mid and rear lock pins, a process that can be performed without tools and which allows the two parts to separate. This basic breakdown, which takes seconds, gives the operator enough access to the gun's vital parts to undertake an essential field clean. A more extensive breakdown can also be performed, depending on the skill levels of the user, and whether or not the degree of maintenance or repair necessary requires the skills of an armorer. Some care needs to

OPPOSITE Here an M82A1's lower receiver (left) and upper receiver (right) are separated, showing features such as the shape of the bolt head and also the two barrel return springs. (Author's photo, © Royal Armouries PR.12187)

OPPOSITE For all their immense reliability, Barrett rifles will sometimes malfunction, often as a result of deficiencies in cleaning or defective ammunition. Here a US soldier attempts to remove a .50-caliber round stuck in the chamber. (US DoD)

be taken because the Barrett, being an immensely powerful weapon, has a correspondingly muscular main spring and barrel springs, held under singing tension. The barrel springs, for example, sit under about 70lb of pressure. Needless to say, anyone disassembling the spring parts of the Barrett needs to ensure that if the springs are accidentally released, there is nobody standing in their potential line of flight.

The Barrett rifle demands the same maintenance rules as almost every other firearm. The US Army's Field Manual FM 3-05.222 *Special Forces Sniper Training* gives concise advice regarding basic field maintenance of the Barrett in its Appendix E:

CLEANING AND LUBRICATION

E-22. The rifle's size makes it relatively easy to clean. The sniper should clean it at the completion of each day's firing or during the day if fouling is causing the weapon to malfunction. He –

• Cleans the bore with rifle bore cleaner (RBC) or a suitable substitute. Each cleaning should include at least six passes back and forth with the bronze-bristle brush, followed by cloth patches until the patches come out clean. Immediately after using bore cleaner, he dries the bore and any parts of the rifle exposed to the bore cleaner and applies a thin coat of oil. He should always clean the bore from the chamber end.

• Cleans the rest of the weapon with a weapons cleaning toothbrush, rags, and cleaning solvent. When using cleaning solvent, he should not expose plastic or rubber parts to it. He dries and lubricates all metal surfaces when clean.

E-23. The sniper should lightly lubricate all exposed metal. These parts are as follows:

• Bolt (locking lugs and cam slot).

• Bolt carrier (receiver bearing surfaces).

• Barrel bolt locking surfaces (receiver bearing surfaces).

• Receiver (bearing surfaces for recoiling parts).

NOTE: The sniper lubricates according to the conditions in the AO. E-24. The sniper should dust off the scope and keep it free of dirt. He should dust the lenses with a lens cleaning brush and only clean them with lens cleaning solvent and lens tissue.

NOTE: The Barrett is easy to maintain, but because of the size of its components the sniper must pay attention to what he is doing, or he may damage the weapon, injure himself, or hurt others around him if not careful. (US Army 2003: E22–E24)

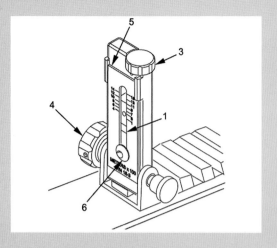
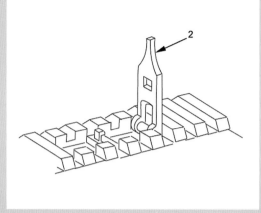

The M107 iron sights, capable of use out to 1,500m (1,640yd): (**1**) sight aperture; (**2**) front post; (**3**) elevation knob; (**4**) windage knob; (**5**) rear sight scale; (**6**) rear sight scale screw. (US Army)

Scopes and suppressors

A Barrett rifle is essentially the hub of a sniper *system*, the totality of the system being comprised of all the technologies that enable the rifle to achieve its long-range accuracy. Of course, the intrinsic precision is utterly wasted if the optics fitted to the rifle are either of poor quality or used incorrectly. The telescopic sights fitted to the Barrett depend on the purpose and preference of the shooter, who has a wide variety of devices to choose from, popular manufacturers being Leupold (the Leupold 4.5×14 Vari-X scope is a standard M107 military fitting), Nightforce, and Schmidt & Bender. Barrett has also recently released a new product to aid the precision shot, namely the Barrett Optical Ranging System (BORS). Essentially, the BORS is a portable ballistic computer that mounts on the rifle scope, attaching directly to the elevation turret. Barrett company website material explains the functioning of the sight:

> BORS instantly takes care of the data work by drawing from several tables and taking into account a number of real-time

external factors so you can focus on the task of achieving first round hits. After determining the range to target, simply turn the elevation knob until the BORS screen matches your target's distance. Internal sensors automatically calculate the ballistic solution. BORS compensates for temperature and barometric pressure, calculates angle cosine and displays rifle cant.

The BORS is very much of the time. While the fundamental nature of firearms still seems resistant to revolution – there are currently no real alternatives to gunpowder-based cartridge weapons – a seminal shift is taking place in sighting systems. For example, the TrackingPoint company of Austin, Texas, has developed a sight that uses "lock-and-launch" technology, automating the ballistic calculation process and enabling (according to company claims) even an inexperienced shot to achieve a first-round hit at long range. The BORS is another system that helps take some of the work out of the most taxing of distance shots.

Barrett M107A1 rifles on display in a Chinese military museum. The gun at the front is fitted with the QDL suppressor, plus a voluminous thermal-imaging scope. (US DoD)

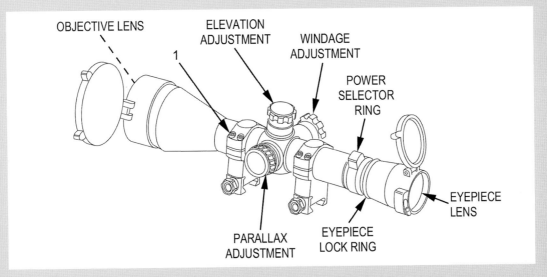

OBJECTIVE LENS

ELEVATION ADJUSTMENT

WINDAGE ADJUSTMENT

POWER SELECTOR RING

EYEPIECE LENS

EYEPIECE LOCK RING

PARALLAX ADJUSTMENT

The Leupold 4.5×14 Vari-X scope, the standard Daylight Scope for US Army M107s, is fitted with a Mildot reticle; and for both windage and elevation 1 click equals a ¼ MOA at 100m (109yd). (US Army)

The BORS is not the only device that can be fitted to a Barrett rifle, and one of particular note is the QDL suppressor. The Barrett, as already noted, is a spectacularly noisy gun, broadcasting its presence for hundreds of meters every time it sends a round down range, and thumping the ears of the shooter and bystanders alike. For hunting and sniping work, therefore, the gun is not exactly the last word in stealth. However, Barrett has produced the QDL suppressor for the M107A1, M99, and M95, which shaves off 23dB from the total report signature, thus helping to tone down the gun's audible presence, but also serving to protect the shooter's hearing.

The suppressor, which measures 12.73in long and weighs 4.88lb, simply slots over the muzzle brakes of the three guns mentioned, then locks in place with a quarter turn and the tightening of a lock ring. The muzzle end of the suppressor can also be fitted with a short auxiliary muzzle brake, to help control the recoil as the main muzzle brake is now masked inside the suppressor. Barrett acknowledges, however, that for optimal flash and noise suppression, the suppressor is best used without the auxiliary brake – but the brake also serves to reduce the impact of the barrel in the receiver upon recoil (the extra mass of the suppressor).

A single-shot bolt-action Barrett M99 fitted with a BORS atop the scope. For tactical durability, the BORS has a minimum 30-hour battery life. (Pink Talon)

The M107 bipod assembly: (**1**) bipod legs; (**2**) bipod locking points; (**3**) lower receiver; (**4**) bipod locking pin, to secure the legs to the receiver. (US DoD)

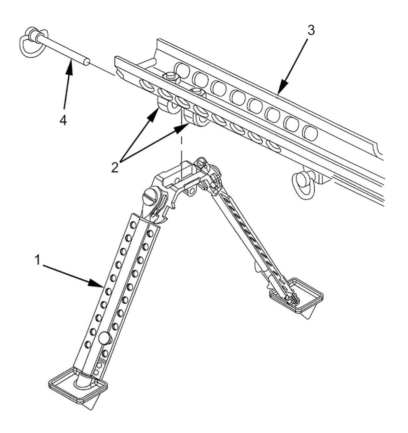

Firing technique

For all the mechanical recoil-compensation features on the Barrett, firing one of these weapons is a sobering experience for the unwary. The recoil is still shoulder thumping and the muzzle blast and report are fearsome. Therefore, those who don't approach the Barrett with respect are in for a rough ride, as this account from US Army Iraq veteran Mark A. Alaimo demonstrates:

> My platoon had just received the .50 cal Barrett sniper rifle. It was a big weapon that could hit anything within our reach. We drove out to a spot that was out of the way and within a mile of one of our regular IP [Iraqi Police] stations. We unloaded the vehicles and set up the Barrett for practice firing. A group of soldiers walked about two hundred meters to a large dirt berm. They finished setting up and walked back to the rest of us. We began firing the large weapon. We covered our ears and could feel the reverberation of the Barrett as the shooter squeezed off a round.
>
> I noticed an IP [Iraqi Policeman] walking in our direction. Most of us tried to ignore his presence as he watched us practice firing the Barrett and adjusting its scope. We fired the weapon in a prone position with it set up on a bipod. We wore two layers of hearing protection to prevent our eardrums from rupturing. While in the prone position, we had to ensure that our feet were dug in, and the butt of the rifle was placed firmly in the pocket of the shoulder. The kick of the Barrett was

so great that if you had a space between the weapon and your shoulder, you were guaranteed a bruise.

The IP's curiosity soon got the best of him, and he asked if he could fire the "big gun," as he put it. We agreed and instructed him on the operation of the weapon. He placed himself in the prone position and shoved the butt of the rifle into his shoulder. I noticed that he wasn't wearing any hearing protection. So I leaned over him and offered earmuffs. He declined, stating that he would be OK without them.

From my personal experience with the Barrett, my hearing would ring with two sets of hearing protection on. The pain that this IP was about to experience was unimaginable. Maybe the equivalent of being next to an IED as it went off. The moment of truth was near as the IP took aim behind the Barrett rifle. He steadied himself, focused his eye behind the scope, and squeezed the trigger.

The recoil of the "big gun" moved the IP backward with such force that he was set on his knees. His hands went straight from the Barrett to his ears. He couldn't hear anything that we were saying. Well, not that we were saying anything, more like laughing hysterically. The IP was trying to laugh with us but he was clearly in pain. (Alaimo 2011)

The position of the M82A1's carrying handle can be adjusted along the length of the mounting rail, allowing the shooter to configure it as a stabilizing foregrip. (Author's photo, © Royal Armouries PR.12187)

With a muzzle report of around 180dB, the Barrett demands that the shooter wears good hearing protection – ideally plugs combined with external ear defenders. (US DoD)

The incident has a certain humor to it, but it would be humane to ask whether the victim suffered any lingering hearing problems. Barrett's official manual for the M107 warns in the clearest of terms that users should ideally wear both earplugs and earmuffs when shooting the gun. It also cautions that

> The muzzle brake is integral to the design of your rifle and works to divert a large portion of a shot's blast rearward and to the side of the muzzle. Your rifle must not be fired without it. People and objects should not be in the vicinity of the muzzle brake because its blast consists of high-pressure and high temperature gas. All spectators should use double hearing protection. The safest place for a spectator is directly behind the shooter. (Barrett 2011: 1)

Handling the gun's recoil correctly is also a key requirement of using the .50-caliber Barrett properly, though the gun does quite a bit of the work for the shooter. As noted, the muzzle brake reduces the felt recoil by around 70 percent – without this, serious damage would likely occur to the shoulders and cheeks of many shooters – and the massive main spring plus the recoil pad also distribute the impact of the recoil significantly. Nevertheless, and as the author can testify, the experience is still salutary.

There are two key requirements for handling the Barrett safely. First, the gun's recoil pad needs to be firmly in the shoulder pocket, with the weight of the upper body leaning forward into the shot, and with no awkward twists in the torso. Any slight gap between shoulder and pad will result in a slamming and bruising impact on the body. Furthermore, a solid engagement between body and gun is important for the smooth operation of the gun's recoil-operated system, because recoil-operated weapons need to push against resistance to ensure that the bolt and barrel recoil faster than the receiver in which they are moving. If the weapon is only loosely shouldered, the receiver's excessive acceleration can maintain pace with the bolt recoil, meaning that the bolt group fails to go through its full recoil cycle, leading to a malfunction. It is the same effect seen when people 'limpwrist' semiautomatic handguns.

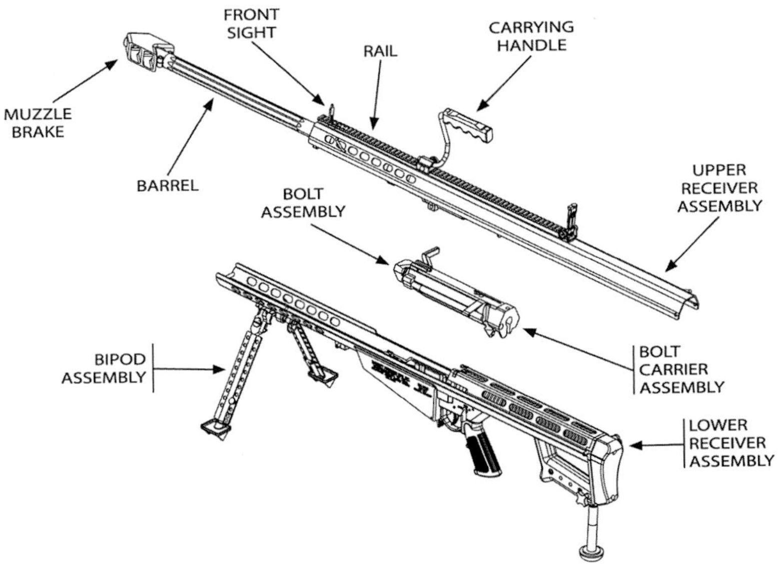

FRONT SIGHT
CARRYING HANDLE
RAIL
MUZZLE BRAKE
BARREL
BOLT ASSEMBLY
UPPER RECEIVER ASSEMBLY
BIPOD ASSEMBLY
BOLT CARRIER ASSEMBLY
LOWER RECEIVER ASSEMBLY

A view of the M107 broken down into its three major assemblies: the upper receiver, bolt group, and lower receiver. (US DoD)

The second important element of safe handling is to maintain a proper eye relief – the distance between the eye and the rear of the telescopic sight. A distance of 3–5in is recommended; anything less than 3in and the shooter is likely to find that the rim of the scope does some serious damage to his eye or forehead.

Ammunition and effects

As part of my research for this book, I watched hours of videos of individuals using Barretts in earnest. This activity produced results that went from the entertaining to the harrowing. The video content ranged from US troops taking long-range sniper shots during action in Afghanistan and Iraq to plucky civilians and service personnel attempting from-the-shoulder standing shots with the rifle, almost all to shrieks of delight from onlookers.

One particular video had a more visceral impact, however. Two hunters in the United States were doing some early-morning deer stalking with a .50-caliber Barrett. The camera played across the shadowy silhouettes of the grazing deer, as the hunters conducted a whispered conversation about which target they would select. After some minutes of deliberation, the choice was made: a sizable female that was presenting itself favorably for the shot. There was a pause, and then the morning stillness was rent apart by the roar of the Barrett.

Two things struck me about what happened next. Although hunters using any appropriate caliber can take down a deer on the spot with a precision shot, a more common outcome is that the deer leaps, staggers, then momentarily recovers and sprints away into cover. The hunter pauses, waits, then eventually makes his way to the impact point to begin the process of tracking the blood trail.

In this case, however, the deer was absolutely poleaxed, its legs buckling and its body instantly slamming into the ground as if driven earthward by a massive unseen hand. This leads me to my second impression. The hunters eventually reached the deer to inspect the damage, which was, with understatement, profound. The exit wound appeared to be feet, not inches, across, as if the animal had been split open in the early stages of poorly judged butchering. The impact was literally *devastating*, explaining in a single glance why the animal was utterly, instantly incapacitated.

I walk the reader through this lurid tale with purpose, for no sensible assessment of how the Barrett has been used in action can be made without an appraisal of its effects on the target. Indeed, the sheer destruction unleashed at point of impact is the very *raison d'être* of the Barrett, combined with its reach.

The starting point for this line of thought is not with the gun itself, but with its ammunition. Like every gun, the Barrett is actually merely a delivery system for ammunition – it is the bullet, not the gun that does the destructive work, although the gun contributes fundamentally to the performance of the round.

There is no better introduction to the sheer power of the .50-caliber round than that provided by Major John Plaster, whose book *Ultimate Sniper* is the most comprehensive single-volume work on the art of sniping. His respect for the .50-caliber is undeniable:

> How can anyone exaggerate .50-caliber performance? Here's a bullet that, even at 1½ miles, crashes into a target with more energy than Dirty Harry's famous .44 Magnum at point-blank. Appreciate the power of this cigar-sized cartridge: the .50 caliber generates up to 25,000 ft-lbs. of muzzle energy, while the .308 M118LR tops out at hardly a tenth of that, just 2,626 ft-lbs., and even the .460 Weatherby Magnum yields "only" 8,095 ft-lbs.
>
> Overpenetration concerns? One custom loader tested his ammo against simulated wooden frame houses and found that his six solid bullets blew completely through six houses – not six walls, six *houses*. (Plaster 2006: 263)

The .50-caliber rounds come in a wide variety of formats, and from an equally wide variety of producers, so a detailed study of each cartridge type is not possible here. However, we should start by acknowledging the cartridge from which all the others are derived: the .50 BMG ball. The .50 BMG was designed at the end of World War I by firearms legend John Browning, the cartridge being specifically created to work in a new generation of heavy machine gun that would become the Browning M2. It is a physically large round, total case length being 3.91in, a bullet weight of around 700 grains, and containing approximately 290 grains of powder.

The standard .50 BMG round is easily capable of chewing through brickwork, wooden planking, sheet steel, and all manner of other urban and natural obstacles. Yet although the common or garden ball ammunition can be used in a Barrett, it rarely is, because such rough-and-ready cartridges do not give the super-accurate flight characteristics required by a precision sniper rifle. Nor does the standard M2 ball round have the anti-materiel capabilities required, especially at long ranges. For these reasons, Barrett users tend to fire a range of match-grade ammunition, which gives them consistent performance and penetration across the Barrett's range spectrum, as well as some of the more physically destructive rounds in the military inventory, such as armor-piercing, tracer, and combinations of the two.

To gain a fuller appreciation of the .50-caliber round when fired from a Barrett, some ammunition data comparisons are useful. It is enlightening, for example, to compare the trajectory and energy-over-range characteristics of the .50-caliber with a typical NATO 7.62mm/.308 sniping round. For this comparison, we will specifically take a

This US sniper team in Iraq is preparing its Barrett rifle to mount upon a tripod, which will provide excellent stability as well as a faster traverse than the standard bipod. (US DoD)

Federal Match .308 Cal.168-grain boat-tail hollowpoint, fired at a muzzle velocity of 8,520ft/sec and zeroed to 91m (100yd). and compare it with Barrett's own .50-caliber ammunition, fired from an M82A1 fitted with a 29in barrel. First we'll look at drop over a 914m (1,000yd) range.

Drop		
Distance (in yards)	7.62mm/.308 drop (in inches)	.50 Barrett drop (in inches)
100	Zero	Zero
200	-4.5	-2.1
300	-15.9	-10
400	-35.5	-24.4
500	-64.6	-46
600	-105	-79.9
700	-159	-115.1
800	-228	-165
900	-315	-227
1,000	-421	-302.8

What we see is the .50 BMG round consistently outperforming the .308 in terms of the depth of its drop over the 1,000yd range, meaning that, in practical terms, the sniper has to work less compensation into his aiming point. The author accepts that real-world sniping is not as simple as this, as much depends upon the type of optics the sniper is using, its zero point, atmospheric conditions, and many other variables. Nevertheless, the table does show the reduced arc of the.50-caliber round's trajectory, partly on account of its heavier bullet. The .50-caliber round is also delivering higher performance due to its greater velocities across the flight range. When the Barrett's round leaves the barrel of the M82A1, it does so at a muzzle velocity of 2,750ft/sec; the .308, leaving a typical 24in barrel, will do so marginally slower at 2,600ft/sec. Observe the velocities maintained across the 1,000yd flight.

Velocities		
Distance (in yards)	7.62mm/.308 velocity (ft/sec)	.50 Barrett velocity (ft/sec)
100	2,420	2,601.9
200	2,240	2,458.6
300	2,070	2,319.9
400	1,910	2.185.6
500	1,760	2,055.7
600	1,610	1,930.4
700	1,480	1,810.1
800	1,360	1,695.2
900	1.260	1,586.2
1,000	1,170	1,438.8

These figures are interesting. They show how the muzzle velocity of the Barrett remains consistently higher than that of the .308 rifle, although this is not surprising given the higher velocity at the muzzle. Over the duration of the 1,000yd flight the .308 loses a total of 1,430ft/sec velocity, while the Barrett loses less at 1,312ft/sec; a marginal difference, but all the more significant when one compares it to the energy delivered by the respective bullets.

Energy delivered		
Distance (in yards)	7.62mm/.308 energy (ft-lb)	.50 Barrett energy (ft-lb)
100	2,180	9,934.7
200	1,870	8,870.6
300	1,600	7,897.8
400	1,355	7,009.7
500	1,150	6,201.3
600	970	5,478.7
700	815	4,803.3
800	690	4,217
900	590	3,692.1
1,000	510	3,230.8

The difference here could not be more pronounced: at 1,000yd, the Barrett round is carrying more than six times the energy of the .308 by virtue of the heavy bullet weight and the still respectable velocity. Even though the Barrett round used is not a specialist armor-piercing type, the power delivered by the bullet over distance clearly illustrates why the .50-caliber Barrett has been type classified as an anti-materiel rifle, while the .308 remains (and respectably so) an anti-personnel rifle.

Of course, the differences in performance reduce somewhat if we look at some of the heavier sniper calibers above 7.62mm/.308. The .338 Lapua Magnum is a case in point, it having been developed in the 1990s as an ultra-long-range cartridge capable of punching through five layers of body armor at 1,000m (1,094yd). Indeed, at the time of writing, the record (although now disputed, see below) for the longest confirmed sniper kill in history goes to Corporal Craig Harrison, Blues and Royals, British Army, who in November 2009 took on a Taliban machine-gun team at a range of 2,475m (2,707yd) using a .338 Accuracy International L115A3 Long Range Rifle. During this astonishing incident, the rifle proved both its anti-personnel and anti-materiel capabilities, with Harrison not only shooting and killing the two machine-gunners, but also destroying the machine gun itself. At a range of 600m (656yd), the .338 round has an energy of 2,624ft-lb, and 1,639ft-lb at 1,000m (1,094yd). These figures are substantially higher than those delivered by the .308, but still well below those relating to the .50-caliber round. Most authorities consider the .338 to be a superb long-range anti-personnel round and a good anti-materiel round for light targets, but not for more resilient obstacles. Even the standard .50-caliber ball ammunition, by contrast, is capable of penetrating 1in of concrete, 6in of sand, and 21in of clay at 1,500m (1,640yd).

US Army soldiers serving with the 1st Battalion, 501st Parachute Infantry Regiment, practice sniping from a UH-60 Black Hawk helicopter, including using a .50-caliber Barrett rifle. The man in the foreground has a 7.62mm M110 Semi Automatic Sniper System. (US DoD)

.50 BMG specifications

Case type: Rimless, bottleneck

Bullet diameter: 0.510in

Neck diameter: 0.560in

Shoulder diameter: 0.714in

Base diameter: 0.804in

Rim diameter: 0.804in

Rim thickness: 0.083in

Case length: 3.91in

Overall length: 5.45in

Case capacity: 292.8 gr H_2O

Primer type: #35 Arsenal Primer

Maximum pressure: 54,800psi

Yet standard ball ammunition is often not the only ammunition of choice for the .50-caliber Barrett sniper. To bolster the weapon's anti-materiel effects, there are a range of other specialist cartridges available. Barrett military users can load up with the M17 tracer round, which although carrying less kinetic energy and accuracy compared to the ball rounds (because of the loss of mass produced by the incendiary component burning in flight), has the ancillary advantage of delivering incendiary effects on flammable targets. To add more penetration to the incendiary effect, the sniper can opt for the Armor-Piercing-Incendiary-Tracer, M20, which has a specially hardened core within its metal jacket. Such a round can slice through 0.75in of steel plate at a range of several hundred yards, and makes short work of even the most hardened bulletproof vests.

In recent years some even more specialist cartridges have emerged on the market for the Barrett (and for other .50-caliber weapons). Two that deserve special mention are the M903 SLAP (Saboted Light Armor Penetrator) and the Mk 211 Mod 0 Raufoss HEIAP (High-Explosive-Incendiary-Armor-Piercing) ammunition. The M903 SLAP round uses the sabot principle to deliver a sub-caliber penetrator at extremely high velocities onto the target. In the SLAP's case, the penetrator is a tungsten bullet of .30 caliber, wrapped in a plastic sabot to take it up to size for firing from a .50-caliber rifle. When separated from its sabot, the penetrator will achieve a maximum velocity of 3,985ft/sec, which gives it the capability to defeat 0.75in of high hard armor at 1,500m (1,640yd); an astonishing capability.

The Mk 211 Mod 0 HEIAP – a multipurpose round developed in the 1970s by the Nordic Ammunition Company (NAMMO) Raufoss AS – is even more advanced. As the full expansion of its HEIAP acronym explains, it combines armor-piercing properties with a high-explosive effect. The round's internal high-explosive charge is detonated by a chain reaction: on impact, the collapse of the bullet's nose cone pyrotechnically ignites an incendiary charge (in itself capable of igniting JP4 and JP8 military jet fuel), which in turn sets off the RDX explosive charge, scattering around 20 potentially lethal fragments at high velocity. Moreover, the sequence of ignition to detonation means that the high-explosive charge goes off with a slight delay, allowing the bullet to achieve penetration before detonating either inside the target or on the other side of it. Penetration figures are 0.43in of 45-degree armor at 1,000m (1,094yd) and (in its AP-S NM173 type) the same depth of armor at 30 degrees at 1,500m (1,640yd). By comparison, a Barrett rifle firing Mk 211 Mod 0 ammunition has a similar destructive capability to that of a 20mm cannon.

The Raufoss round is a sobering piece of ammunition, and it has attracted some controversy. In the late 1990s, the International Committee of the Red Cross began conducting tests on the Mk 211, arguing that the round contravened the 1868 St. Petersburg Declaration that prohibited the use of exploding or incendiary rounds with bullets weighing less than

14oz against human targets. The full complexities of this case will not be examined here, but in summary the Mk 211 was judged as legal, principally because anti-personnel use was not its intended role (although it was accepted that a sniper might have to take such a shot depending on the tactical situation, especially if he didn't have time to switch the type of ammunition in his gun), and that most of the time the rounds, when fired into humans, didn't actually detonate until the cartridge had passed through the unfortunate victims.

THE BARRETT'S ROLES

Given the aforementioned exploration of the Barrett's ammunition types, we can now look more closely at the definition of the rifle's specific battlefield roles. A useful way into this discussion is to quote from the US Army's FM 3-05.222 *Special Forces Sniper Training and Employment*, in its description of the "Role Of The M82A1 Caliber .50 SWS":

E-1. The military can use the M82A1 in several different roles – as the long-range rifle, the infantry support rifle, and the explosive ordnance disposal tool. Personnel use the M82A1 as –

• A long-range rifle to disable valuable targets that are located outside the range or the capabilities of conventional weapons, many times doing so in situations that may preclude the use of more sophisticated weapons.
• An infantry support rifle to engage lightly armored vehicles and to penetrate light fortifications that the 5.56 mm and the 7.62 mm cannot defeat.
• An explosive ordnance disposal tool to engage and disrupt several types of munitions at ranges from 100 to 500 meters. In most cases, the munitions are destroyed or disrupted with a single hit and without a high-order detonation.

E-2. When used in any of its roles, the caliber .50 SWS and personnel trained to use it are vital assets to the commander. In light of this, a training program is necessary to maximize their potential. (US Army 2003: E1–E2)

These students at the Royal Dutch Marine Sniper Instruction School are surrounded by a variety of sniper weapons, including the Barrett M82A1 and M99 (side by side, in the middle ground) and the Accuracy International AWM-F (beige stocks). (US DoD)

It is worth looking at these roles in a little more detail, and to bring in some real-world examples (primarily during the recent "War on Terror" in Iraq and Afghanistan) by way of elucidation. At the same time, we will absorb some of the practical and tactical challenges of the Barrett as a battlefield weapon.

The long-range shot

We have already become familiar with the concept of the .50-caliber Barrett as a "long-range rifle," but this needs to be explored in greater detail. First, what exactly do we mean by "long range"? Here we have to distinguish between the optimal range characteristics of the weapon and the practical sniping capabilities of the user. Historical precedent since the late 1980s has shown us that Barrett rifles are consistently capable of taking on point targets at distances of 1,500m (1,640yd) and beyond, and larger area or object targets out to 2,500m (2,734yd). Yet saying that such distant engagements are common does not mean that they are in any way straightforward – we must always remember that for every hit there will likely be an equal or greater number of misses at ranges that are on the very edge of the visual spectrum.

At distances beyond the 1,500m (1,640yd) mark, the sniper faces a range of profound challenges to the shot, even when armed with a rifle with the long arms of a Barrett. He, or a spotter working alongside him, has to see and identify the target in the first place, often among complicated and blending terrain features. (Note that the spotters will often be equipped with super-powerful spotter scopes, with magnifications in the region of 30× to acquire the target.) With a scope of at least 10× magnification minimum, the sniper should be able to identify the basic characteristics of the figure, including whether or not he has a weapon; beyond that, magnifications of 14–20× are required to make the shot feasible.

The sniper then needs to make a range estimation, and one that is highly accurate. For example, at 1,370m (1,500yd) a range estimation that is inaccurate by just 68.5m (75yd) will result in the bullet falling

Accurate distance calculation for long-range Barrett shots can be problematic in mountainous areas, where terrain features and strange perspectives can confuse standard methods of ranging. Laser rangefinders are therefore a welcome addition. (US DoD)

many feet long or short of the target. Thankfully for modern long-range snipers, technological support is at hand in the form of laser rangefinders (LRFs). Such instruments are impressively accurate, and they have the advantage that unlike conventional methods of manual range estimation, they do not rely on possibly inaccurate assumptions about relative object heights at distance. All it takes to use such a system, typically, is to focus it on the target, press a button, and look at the readout panel. (LRFs can be either separate devices or they can be mounted to the rifle itself with fixtures such as the M107 Electro-Optics Mount, which enables an LRF to be fitted on the rail under the day optical sight.) Professional and properly trained snipers, however, will understand the limitations of the laser rangefinder, particularly when taking a very-long-range shot with a Barrett. One factor that can interfere with an LRF is atmospheric scintillation,

A spotter makes range calculations. The spotting scope on the tripod is the popular Leupold Mk 4 12–40×60mm. (US DoD)

in which variations in air density between the LRF and the target distort and bend the laser beam, giving an inaccurate reading from another object around the target. Another factor is that if the sniper is using the LRF close to the ground, and the landscape between him and the target inclines at a shallow angle, the laser can "graze" small landscape features in front of the target, again producing an inaccurate reading. A similar problem can occur if the target is set against a complicated, poorly defined backdrop, as it becomes difficult to lock onto the target with precision. In the war in Afghanistan, this could be a particular problem when operating in mountainous regions, with humans moving among subtle, variegated backdrops of rock, low-level brush, and scree. Another issue for the long-range shooter is that while the target itself might be big enough to see reasonably clearly, there might be other objects in the path of the laser that aren't visible at the extreme ranges involved, such as leaves and branches. In Iraq, and during the hot summer months in Afghanistan, there is the additional problem of heat mirage interfering with the visual acquisition and lazing of the target.

For all these reasons, advanced technology is never regarded as a replacement for fundamental sniping knowledge about range estimation, although technology is likely to become a substitute for marksmen who haven't been through the advanced ballistics instruction of full sniper training. FM 3-05.222 also gives the following advice for the M107 sniper:

When in doubt of range estimation, aim low and adjust using the sight-to-burst method. Second shots are frowned upon with a 7.62 SWS because of two things – the target getting into a prone position (which most people do when shot at) and the sniper revealing his position. Neither of these principles apply to the caliber .50 SWS when it is used against armored or fortified targets. Armored personnel carriers (APCs) cannot "duck," nor is an enemy buttoned into a bunker or an

Indonesian Marines are familiarized with the M82A1 SASR. High-quality scope rings are essential, gripping the scope tight but without applying any distortion to the scope body. (USMC)

APC as observant as he could be. The sniper needs to have carefully observed his area before assuming the above to be always true. (US Army 2003: E1–E2)

The sight-to-burst method is essentially that of "walking" the rounds onto the target, which the writer of the manual acknowledges is applicable to the M107 when used in its primary anti-materiel role. However, even if the rifle is used against individual human targets, the method can have relevance. At very long ranges, those being shot at might not hear any muzzle report from the gun, particularly if they are surrounded by significant levels of ambient noise. Thus if they do not actually see or hear the impacts near them, they might be completely unaware of death incrementally moving closer.

Moving back to the rifle itself, the scope also needs to be capable of handling the elevation required to compensate for bullet drop. Think back to the figures relating to bullet drop presented earlier. With a rifle zeroed to 91m (100yd), the .50-caliber round will drop 7.62m (25ft) at 914m (1,000yd) – more than four times greater than the height of an average human. The drop effect intensifies as the range stretches further, as the bullet loses momentum and the rate of drop to earth increases. At 1,829m (2,000yd), therefore, the bullet drop will be a massive 35.40m (116ft), and that is in perfect sea-level conditions.

Not that the Barrett is incapable of taking such shots, at least from a mechanical and ballistic point of view. For a shot out to 2,000yd, the sniper will need a scope that has at least 120 MOA of elevation adjustment. The classic Barrett US military scope – the Leupold Mk 4 M1 10× – has a maximum elevation of 90 MOA, while the 16× version has 140 MOA. Some Marine snipers use a Unertl 10× scope with a special bullet-drop compensator (BDC) feature, which allows the user to take shots out to 2,000yd. It should also be noted that the Barrett optics rails on the M107 are tapered by 27 MOA, meaning that the rail can add 27 MOA to the rifle's scope elevation, enabling those super-long-range shots without cramming the target picture all the way to the bottom of the sight reticle.

Taking account of bullet drop is demanding enough, but it is just one of several factors to consider. Even at high velocities, the .50 BMG bullet will still take a significant length of time to reach the target at extreme ranges – 2.5 seconds at 1,372m (1,500yd) and 4.5 seconds at 1,829m

OPPOSITE A US serviceman holds the correct eye relief on a Barrett M107. Note how he has taped range information to the upper receiver. (US DoD)

US 101st Airborne, Southern Baghdad, Iraq, 2005 (previous pages)

A US Army sniper with the 502nd Infantry Regiment, 101st Airborne Division, takes up position on a rooftop, armed with an M82A1 and accompanied by a spotter equipped with an M151 Improved Spotting Scope, looking for targets over the cityscape. The spotter's relationship with the sniper is integral; the two men operate as one unit, with the spotter relaying target information and shot-adjustment advice to the shooter. Tripod mounted, the M151 features a 12–40× magnification, with a 60mm objective lens diameter plus a Leupold MilDot reticle for range estimation. Although the Barrett's range might be considered excessive given the relatively close ranges in an urban zone, in Iraq it was ideal for both anti-vehicle overwatch (i.e. stopping vehicle-borne suicide bombers by a shot to the engine block), for destroying IEDs at a safe distance, and for striking human targets behind typical cover, especially concrete or block walls. At ranges of around 200m (218yd) the Barrett's .50-caliber rounds will punch through most standard concrete cinder blocks.

(2,000yd). During this flight, the bullet will be subject to environmental effects such as wind and rain, the interference of which must be factored into the sniper's calculation. An incorrect judgment of wind direction, by just 10–15 degrees, even applied to a fairly sedate wind of just a few miles per hour, can result in a miss by the width of the human being. The sniper will also have to make adjustments for headwinds (which require an increase in elevation on account of the greater drag on the bullet and therefore its more rapidly decreasing velocity), and a decrease in elevation for a tailwind (for the opposite reasons).

The list of issues goes on and on. Air pressure either from weather or temperature, for example, will affect the velocity and therefore the trajectory of a bullet; the denser the air, the slower the flight to the target. Taking air pressure into account has been particularly relevant for snipers operating in Iraq, as the hot desert temperatures and thin equatorial air result in flatter trajectories and faster flight times. Major John Plaster also notes that even the spinning of the earth needs to be taken into account at the extreme ranges made possible by a .50-caliber rifle:

> Time of flight also relates to the rotational speed of the earth. In one single day – one earth rotation – the planet turns approximately 25,000 miles at the equator, which equates to 1,042 mph, or 1,531 fps, with slightly less relative speed as you approach the poles. Your bullet's speed will vary a tiny amount, depending on whether you're shooting with or against the earth's rotation or angled away from the equator. It's a tiny, tiny amount, but its influence, too, grows with distance. (Plaster 2006: 274)

Thankfully for the modern sniper, there are now handheld computerized devices that can make ballistic judgments with total accuracy in a matter of milliseconds. In 2008–09, both the US Marine Corps and the US Army placed orders for significant quantities (1,000 and 6,500 respectively) of Advanced Ballistic Calculators (ABCs), these being special handheld computers made by Horus Vision. The ATragMX ballistics software automatically calculates the effects of all environmental factors affecting

This diagram from the US Army's M107 manual shows the full rifle kit as it is delivered to the front-line soldier. (US Army)

MAGAZINES

DEPLOYMENT KIT CLEANING KIT OPTICAL CLEANING KIT

the flight of the bullet to target, the software also being matched to the particular gun and caliber being used. Allied to a rifle like the Barrett, the ABC provides invaluable and accurate data for shots out to 2,500m (2,734yd) and beyond. The Barrett BORS system mentioned earlier also can make a dramatic difference to the placement of the shot.

Further technological support for the Barrett shot can come from other larger unit surveillance kit. Many US Army Scout vehicles, for example, are mounted with the Raytheon Long Range Advanced Scout Surveillance System (LRAS3), which according to company literature provides "the real-time ability to detect, recognize, identify and geo-locate distant targets," doing so by a utilizing a mixture of forward-looking infrared (FLIR) detectors and global positioning system (GPS) designation. In the following account, written up in the US *1st Infantry Division News* following the battle of Fallujah, Iraq, we see how hi-tech surveillance and the Barrett can come together with devastating effect:

> Once in position and looking west down into the city, the scouts used their Long Range Advanced Scout Surveillance System (LRAS3) – a device that uses thermal imaging to register heat signatures – to call for fire on targets deep into the city in preparation for the main push.
>
> Later in the day (8 Nov.) the troops began receiving sniper fire. As Spc. James Taylor scanned the city through the LRAS3, he spotted another sniper in a window about 1,200 meters [1,312yd] out.
>
> Corporal Omar Torres, an infantryman and sniper from the 2nd Battalion, 2nd Infantry Scout Platoon, joined the men on the road, bringing with him his .50 caliber M107 sniper rifle. With Taylor acting as his spotter, he sent several rounds into the building.
>
> "Oh man, you nailed him," shouted Taylor who was still watching through the LRAS3. (Snow 2007)

This account makes an important contribution to our understanding of the Barrett rifle in action. Precisely *because* of its ability to take shots out

This Marine's final firing position (FFP) utilizes natural cover perfectly, virtually surrounding him with protective rock faces. Note the full camo finish to all parts of the gun, including the scope. (US DoD)

to such long ranges, it is often integrated into a broader spectrum of technological assets, from LRFs to advanced surveillance and detection systems. Taking shots out to more than 2,000m (2,187yd) stretches the capacity of human senses and accuracy to the absolute limit, so for the extreme shots Barrett shooters will generally rely upon every technological asset available.

The role that luck can also play in hitting targets at the extremes of the Barrett's range should never be underestimated. Nor should it be assumed that such shots are not problematic in the extreme, affected by the many variables outlined above, plus numerous other technological factors. Sometimes problems with accuracy might not even be the fault of the weapon at all, but of the ammunition it delivers down range. For example, on November 20, 2012, the *Marine Corps Times* reported complaints from the field in Afghanistan from scout snipers, who were facing a specific accuracy challenge. One method of ambush used by the Taliban in Afghanistan is to launch an assault rifle or sniper attack via a relatively small hole (typically about 15in diameter) cut through the earthen walls that lace the country's rural hinterland. The *MCT* report found that many scout snipers alleged that the Mk 211 Raufoss round (the A606 in official Marine terminology) was failing to give them the consistent accuracy required to put rounds through the hole and into the enemy at long ranges. As one Marine noted:

> The hits that our platoon has recorded out to 1,500 meters [1,640yd] using the A606 have required the sniper to fire multiple shots on one target in order to "walk" the rounds on to the target [the "sight-to-burst" method outlined previously] … This is a waste of ammunition and it compromises the sniper's position by giving the enemy multiple rounds with which to locate the sniper's hide. (Lamothe 2012)

The author is unable to comment on the validity of this particular claim – as we shall see, the Mk 211 seems to have gained a good reputation in many other contexts – but it does at least highlight the critical role ammunition plays in realizing the full potential of a good rifle.

It should also be remembered that the scope on the rifle, and the shooter's ability to handle it properly, also largely defines the capability of the gun itself. The finest gun in the world will be let down by either poor optics or a scope that is not appropriate for the demands placed upon it. The subtleties of this relationship between gun and sight are brought out in a US report entitled: *Operation Iraqi Freedom: PEO Soldier Lessons Learned* (2003). In the report, the author comments on reports from the field about both the scope fitted to the XM107 and the spotter sights:

> The most pervasive negative comment was that snipers felt the Leupold Sight was inadequate for the weapon – that it was not ballistically matched. If the sight was zeroed for 500, 1000 and 1500 meters, soldiers did not feel confident in their ability to engage targets at the "between" distances (e.g. 1300 m). Snipers felt there were better sights available for this weapon such as the Swarovski. Sniper team spotters felt the tripod for the Leupold Spotter Scope could be better designed. COL Bray, Commander, 2d BCT, 82d Airborne Division supported an Operational Needs Statement for a Sniper Sight that would allow the sniper to identify targets as combatants or non-combatants out to 2000m. (Smith 2003: 3)

Again, the present author withholds judgment on this perceived problem, having never personally engaged combat targets with any scope in the field. What it does indicate is that a sniper rifle like the Barrett is only as good as its supporting parts. The ability to deliver an accurate shot is the result of the coordination of rifle, ammunition, scope, sniper, and environment – hence tracking down the root problem of off-target shots is no simple matter. What can be said with full confidence, however, is that the Barrett has proven itself time and time again as being capable of reaching out to targets accurately when other rifles run out of steam.

While talking about long-range Barrett shooting, and having mentioned the world record shot of Corporal Harrison, it should be noted that there are unconfirmed reports this record has now been broken by none other than the Barrett M82A1, in service with the Australian Army. In October 2012, the global press began recounting an incident in which an Australian 2 Commando Regiment sniper team spotted a group of Taliban fighters through binoculars. They took range calculations, which came out at a prodigious 2,815m (3,078yd), nearly 400m (437yd) farther than Harrison's engagement range. Two of the team were armed with M82A1 rifles (details about the scopes and ammunition used are unavailable), and decided to take the shot. According to the press reports, both men fired simultaneously. After a six-second flight time, one of the Taliban fell dead under a .50-caliber impact, although apparently neither sniper could claim for sure whose bullet had hit the mark.

With professional confidentiality, the Australian armed services have neither confirmed nor denied the reports, although the details we know are certainly plausible. Whatever the truth, we can recognize that while the stated range of the shot is extreme, even for the Barrett, it would still be perfectly possible (with massive elevation) for the sniper to reach out to this distance.

Not to scale

US Marine Corps, Afghanistan, 2012 (previous pages)

The conflict in Afghanistan since 2001 has seen the widespread use of long-range sniper rifles such as the Barrett. Records for the longest sniper kill have fallen repeatedly during the conflict, and the current unconfirmed record (2,815m/3,078yd) belongs to a Barrett M82A1 in the hands of Australian Army forces. Here, however, a US Marine Corps scout sniper takes aim through a Leupold Mk 4 LR/T scope atop a Barrett M82A3, focusing on a Taliban target in Afghanistan during the summer months of 2012. The silhouette diagram (top left) illustrates the realities of trajectory a sniper has to negotiate over long ranges. Contrary to popular belief, rifle bullets fly in a parabolic arc from the muzzle rather than flat. Therefore, if the sight were aligned parallel to the barrel for medium- or long-range shots, the round would drop markedly low, as illustrated in the upper rifle. To avoid this happening, the sniper adjusts the scope so that the bullet drops onto the target at the point of aim (lower rifle). As illustrated in the inset image, the sniper can also use the Leupold Mildot sight to adjust for both elevation and windage; here the sniper is allowing for drop and for a strong wind from the right, although he could also adjust his scope so that the crosshairs sit centrally on the target.

Effects on target

In 1991, as already noted, the US Marine Corps took the step of acquiring a small batch of Barrett rifles and training up a dedicated group of snipers in their use, in preparation for the forthcoming *Desert Storm* operation. (Some sources state that 40 US Army snipers also received instruction in using the Barrett, something the author has been unable to confirm at the time of writing.) Correctly sensing that they would need weapons with ultra-long range, the USMC trained up some 90 snipers in using the M82A1, and put them into action against the Iraqi Army.

The results were compelling. The destructive force and long range of the Barrett meant that the Marine snipers were able to step out beyond their usual anti-personnel role, and take on enemy assets that would have usually been tackled by heavy weapons. For example, during the period February 23–28 a USMC Surveillance Targeting Acquisition Platoon conducted harrying operations using Barrett rifles against an entire Iraqi mechanized brigade, hitting vehicles and personnel from ranges out to 1,463m (1,600yd), and causing panic among the enemy ranks. Sniper specialist Martin Pegler provides similar narratives from the Gulf War in his book *Out of Nowhere*, and gives one particular example of how the Barrett's .50-caliber round can take on some substantial vehicles:

> Used by Special Forces to neutralise aircraft, radio and radar equipment, and even AFVs, in the hands of a good shot these rifles proved a fearsome battlefield tool as Sergeant Kenneth Terry, 3rd/1st Marines proved. Firing his Barrett at a range in excess of 1,200 yards (1,100 metres) he stopped two Iraqi YW531 armoured personnel carriers, quite literally in their tracks, by firing two rounds of armour-piercing/ incendiary ammunition. If this doesn't seem very remarkable, consider that in desert conditions heat haze, unpredictable vortexes caused by hot air and strong winds, can make even close-range shots hard to calculate and even more difficult to achieve. (Pegler 2006: 322–23)

In any (albeit rather callous) cost-benefit analysis, the Barrett delivers an extraordinarily disproportionate effect for its ammunition expenditure. Reflect here on the fact that two YW 531 APCs, each costing in the region of $600,000 on the international market, were destroyed by several .50-caliber rounds costing a few dollars each.

This photo perfectly captures the swirling dust cloud kicked up by the Barrett's muzzle brake. Dampening the ground with water before firing can help reduce the visual signature. (US DoD)

So just how effective is the Barrett in its anti-materiel role? Although some penetration figures for various .50-caliber rounds are given above when looking at ammunition types, these figures need to be made more meaningful. In the Gulf War, and during the early months of the coalition invasion of Iraq in 1991, the principal vehicular targets for the Barrett sniper teams were civilian cars, SUVs and trucks plus their military-spec equivalents, and light armored vehicles. Regarding the light vehicles, the Barrett has absolutely no problem dealing with almost any component part. Even just the standard ball rounds will carve through doors, glass, and body panels with casual ease, often passing right through the vehicle, and will do so at long ranges. Of course, leaving a huge hole in a door panel is dramatic, but won't stop the vehicle in its tracks. There are two principal means of stopping a vehicle: destroy its engine or eliminate the occupants. In terms of engine destruction, John Plaster, in a review of the Barrett rifle in *American Rifleman*, conducted some tests with Barrett-made ball rounds. Firing three rounds at a V-6 engine block, for example, he found that each of the rounds punched through the block's thick metal exterior, and one even went right through the entire block, exiting from the other side. Given the sheer metallic strength and mass of an engine block, Plaster's test is a stunning demonstration of the weapon's power, and perfectly illustrates the Barrett's anti-materiel potential.

Looking at heavier vehicles, the Barrett is generally incapable of immobilizing a tank or one of the heavier breeds of infantry fighting vehicle (although it can make a mess of items like vision blocks and communications antennae), but it is capable of taking on many APCs and light armored cars. This was proven during both *Desert Storm* and in the invasion of Iraq in 2003. In 2003, for example, the Iraqi Army's mechanization was heavily reliant upon the Soviet-era BMP-series vehicles (it had 900 in its fleet). At its thickest, the BMP armor is 23mm (0.9in) deep, not allowing for the deepening effect of its slant, and with AP rounds

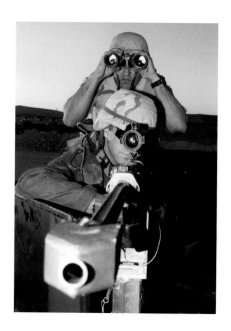

A USAF sniper and spotter scan carefully for targets, the Barrett M82A1 fitted to a pintle mount on an armored vehicle. The troops belong to an EOD unit, and are using the Barrett to destroy explosive devices from a safe range. (USAF)

the Barrett is capable of going through that depth at 200m (219yd). At 600m (656yd), the Barrett would start to struggle with both the hull and turret armor, but it could defeat the armor of other lighter vehicles such as the BMD, BTR-60, BRDM-2, and MTLB.

Beyond vehicles, the Barrett is also capable of destroying a variety of physical objects and structures. Look around any city block, and you will see virtually nothing that wouldn't be undone by the Barrett's impact. John Plaster, following on from his pulverizing of the V-6 engine block, went on to tackle 8×8×12in concrete blocks; the rounds "totally blew out the back, shattering and crumbling the blocks. No barricaded gunman could withstand such a fusillade fired against the concrete or brick wall that concealed him, and Iraq's mud-brick structures offer even less protection" (Plaster 2008). This test reveals why the Barrett is also a useful weapon in close-range urban warfare, as it can be applied almost as a form of light support artillery against structures more resistant to the fire of standard infantry weapons. At 91m (100yd), for example, a Barrett-fired AP round will defeat 9in of concrete, 96in of timber, 1.8in of steel, 20in of rubble, 28in of dry soil, and 42in of wet soil (Plaster 2006: 275). These penetration figures mean that a Barrett team can take on virtually any type of adopted or improvised cover, such as barricades made from assorted rubble or heavy walls. Remember also that the sniper can put multiple rounds into the material surface, the bullets progressively "eating" their way through to the other side.

Although the Barrett is classified as an AMR, it must also be acknowledged that the rifle is frequently used directly against individual human targets. Typically this is because the target is too far away to be tackled by an ordinary rifle, or because a target of opportunity presents itself to a Barrett crew. Given the description provided earlier of the unfortunate deer shot by a Barrett, the effects of the round on a human being are naturally horrifying. One sniper of the 325th Parachute Infantry Regiment described shooting an Iraqi fighter in 2003, and noted: "My spotter positively identified a target at 1400 meters [1,531yd] carrying an RPG on a water tower. I engaged the target. The top half of the torso fell forward out of the tower and the lower portion remained in the tower" (quoted in Haskew 2012). Such profound tissue destruction is commonly reported by Barrett operators – use of the word "disintegrated" is not unusual. Yet in the grim calculus of war, this physical horror can serve a purpose. Lieutenant Colonel Jim Smith, author of the *Operation Iraqi Freedom: PEO Soldier Lessons Learned* document quoted earlier, notes that "Leaders and scouts viewed the effect of the 50 cal round as a combat multiplier due to the psychological impact on other combatants that viewed the destruction of the target" (Smith 2003: 3). Simply put, if the person next to you suddenly exploded, and did so as a result of the impact of a bullet fired from beyond visual range, your most likely natural instinct would be to find cover and to stay in it.

A member of the Missouri National Guard fires an M107, delivering 400m (437yd) demonstration shots for soldiers of the Japanese Ground Self-Defense Force. Note how the grip on the underside of the stock locks his body into a stable firing position. (US DoD)

TACTICAL CONSIDERATIONS

In talking about the tactical potential of the Barrett, due care must be given to distinguish the general tactical applications of all sniper weapons from the specific considerations applied to the Barrett. Snipers as a group are united in a set of common roles: inflict attrition upon enemy personnel (and materiel, if the weapon is capable); impose restrictions on enemy movement; provide overwatch security; and conduct reconnaissance and observation (an important role that is often overlooked). Snipers must perform these roles with stealth, intelligence, and ruthlessness. Much of their focus is on simply getting into the best final firing position (FFP), a challenge that can take many hours of covert movement, and then conducting an escape from enemy attentions once they have taken the shot.

Barrett snipers share these concerns and objectives with all other snipers. Yet the Barrett is a distinctive weapon among the sniper community, both in its physical properties and its tactical potential, and so it needs a separate evaluation.

First, it is useful to explain some of the Barrett's limitations, and foremost among these is its heavy weight. The Barrett is not a gun to sling casually onto a shoulder or to carry silently while crawling through foliage to a shooting position. In fact, the Barrett's weight generally means that it is often only deployable by vehicle (or by particularly strong and long-suffering troops over short distances). The vehicle's security, therefore, has to be incorporated into the sniper team's tactical thinking, especially if the team wants to achieve covert emplacement. In many ways, the Barrett has to be treated like a light crew-served weapon. In US military service, the Barrett typically has a three-man team: shooter, spotter, and security. While a single "lone wolf" sniper with a standard sniper rifle is highly maneuverable, and can occupy concealed hides, the Barrett team is slower to move and set up and is thus potentially more visible to the enemy. Whatever position the team occupies, it has to allow not only for the dimensions of the gun, but also for the position of the team members. In a standard sniper/spotter orientation, the spotter will simply sit or lie alongside the sniper, to align himself with the sniper's shot. The Barrett's spotter, however, needs to be aware of the intense blast that will drive out and back from the muzzle brake, and so he puts himself at a safe distance or angle to avoid potential injury.

The muzzle blast of the Barrett creates other issues for the team. A critical objective for professional snipers is to stay unidentified to the enemy as much as possible, even after taking a shot, because as soon as a sniper's position is unmasked, it will generally attract heavy retaliatory gunfire. The Barrett's post-shot visibility is generally high compared to many other sniper rifles. Not only is the report extremely loud (about 180dB), but the kick-up of dust and dirt upon firing can create a swirling cloud around the shooter – particularly so when operating in very dry, dusty conditions, and if the shooter is firing from the prone position with the muzzle close to the ground – that is visible from distance. Therefore the Barrett sniper team has to think very carefully about the tactical outcomes of taking a shot, especially if they are within a few hundred yards of the enemy.

The US Army field manual FM 3-05.222 includes an entire Appendix devoted to the applications of the M82A1 in combat. At the time of its publication (2003), it was evident that the Barrett was still bedding itself down tactically into military thinking:

> However, even after having been deployed to operational units, no comprehensive training plan has been developed to train snipers on this new role. The basic approach to the large-bore sniper rifle has been that it is nothing more than a big M24 (7.62-mm sniper rifle). This logic has its obvious flaws. Many of the techniques learned by the sniper need to be modified to compensate for this new weapon system. Some of these changes include movement techniques, maintenance requirements, sniper team size and configuration, support requirements, and the marksmanship skills necessary to engage targets at ranges in excess of 1,800 meters [1,969yd]. To keep up with the battles fought in-depth, as well as smaller-scale conflicts, the need for a sniper trained and equipped with a large-bore rifle is apparent. (US Army 2003: E1)

The author of the manual is acutely aware that the Barrett sits in a different tactical and technological category to other sniper weapons, and should be treated accordingly. The manual goes on to make some firmer recommendations:

> Conduct movement into or occupy an FFP with the M82A1 SWS. Sniper should -
>
> Modify his movement techniques to accommodate for the following:
> • Increased weight of the system, ammunition, and team equipment.
> • Better route selection (amount of crawling is reduced).
> • Better selection of withdrawal routes (after the shot, the sniper becomes a higher-priority target and must select route for quick egress).
>
> Occupy an FFP and adjust for the following:
> • Much larger signature to front, clear area and dampen soil [to reduce the dust cloud on firing].

- Signature also at 65 degrees, fan to right and left of sniper.
- Size requirement for a 3-man sniper team in a permanent hide may make it unfeasible for many applications.
- FFP should prevent long-range "skylined" targets. (US Army 2003: E3–E4)

Reading through this list of considerations, it might seem that the Barrett's demands make it a rather cumbersome weapon that taxes the sniper teams both physically and in terms of tactical dexterity. To draw such a conclusion, however, would be to miss two vital points. First, the Barrett sniper team is part of a wider force – it is rarely left on its own in isolation to live or die by its own means. Instead it works within the supportive environment of a multi-arms team, with infantry, vehicle, and even air assets providing protection and therefore greater operational freedom. Second, we come back to the Barrett's range. Because of its long-range capability, the Barrett can be emplaced a relatively safe distance from the enemy, and the distance in itself reduces the team's detectability and allows them to establish survivable final firing positions. Of course, the main operational context of the Barrett in the "War on Terror" has been with professional Western armies fighting against determined insurgent forces equipped with low-level technology. Were the Barrett teams to be faced with very modern opponents, who had access to better surveillance, detection, and long-range response systems, doubtless the tactics would also have to be modified and adjusted.

OPERATIONS

When looking at specific operations conducted by Barrett teams, what strikes home is the flexibility of the weapon. The Barrett's long range enables it to attack distant opponents, who are often operating in places they believe are beyond the reach of enemy fire – until the rounds start thudding in. Thus the Barrett rifle not only extends the security overwatch distance it can provide to other troops, but also imposes attrition and movement restrictions on enemy troops and vehicles well before they can reach conventional small-arms engagement distances of roughly 300m (328yd). A coordinated team of Barretts can provide cover and heavy suppressive fire to an infantry advance, or smash up enemy defenses in an urban zone prior to an assault. Barretts can also be used when the enemy

The versatility of the Barrett means that it has been distributed throughout the US armed services. Here a US Navy aviation ordnanceman fires an M107 off the fantail of the aircraft carrier USS *John C. Stennis* during a live-fire exercise in the western Pacific. (US DoD)

is hiding behind cover, the .50-caliber rounds biting through any sort of wall, eventually either forcing those behind the cover to flee (and thereby expose themselves to other sources of fire) or face being killed or wounded as the bullets eventually pass through the wall.

Sometimes the Barrett operators work in a slightly mundane role, occupying a dusty position for hours and scanning the landscape continually through scope and binoculars to identify and respond to emerging threats. Other times, however, they are integrated into a specific wider battle plan. A good example of the latter is seen in operations conducted by US forces in southern Afghanistan in 2010, specifically against the Taliban stronghold of Zhari District, 20.5 miles west of Kandahar. The plan was to launch a major operation (codenamed Operation *Dragoon Strike*) to clear enemy forces from around the vital Highway 1, a main artery for International Security Assistance Forces (ISAF) in the region. A sub-operation within this plan was Operation *Nashville I*, in which US infantry and air-assault troops would take and hold some key strategic points, including a compound named Observation Post (OP) Dusty, which would be taken by a scout platoon consisting of three 5–6-man reconnaissance teams plus a sniper section of nine men, the latter being divided into three three-man teams. The weapon and equipment composition of the platoon was as follows:

> Each scout packed 32 20-ounce bottles of water, eight MREs (Meals Ready to Eat), and 20 empty sandbags. Most were armed with M4 rifles with attached M203 grenade launchers. Some had M14 Enhanced Battle Rifles and three men were equipped with M249 Squad Automatic Weapon (SAW) machine guns. Squad leaders used M320 grenade launchers while the snipers carried either the M107 Barrett or M24 sniper rifle. To provide extra firepower, Faucher had two of the sniper teams each carry an M240B medium machine gun with tripod and ammunition. He also added four AT4 anti-armor weapons to the platoon's arsenal. Each man also had between 240 and 270 rounds of rifle ammunition. "We had a lot of extra ammunition;" said Faucher, "because I had a feeling it was going to be a fight." (Wright 2010: 160)

The firepower carried by this one platoon represents a broad swathe of the firepower spectrum, from the short-range, quick-fire capability of the 5.56mm M4 through to the long-range power of the M107 and the M240B. It was clear that the platoon meant business.

The operation was launched in the early-morning hours of September 26, with the scout platoon deployed some distance from the objective via a US Army CH-47 Chinook helicopter. Once the helicopter had departed after deploying the scout platoon, the troops then faced a grueling three-and-a-half-hour march across tough terrain to the objective, which they then cleared and prepared for a defense. The terrain around them was flat, but complicated by grape fields, numerous walls, trees and shrubs, and various other features that provided the enemy with lines of approach.

The Taliban soon responded, and OP Dusty became the focal point of an incredibly intense engagement, enemy fire coming from every conceivable angle. The snipers had particularly tough work to do, as the enemy would appear only fleetingly between cover. Author Kevin M. Hymel captures the intensity of the firefight, and the role of the .50-caliber rifles in it:

Transporting the Barrett the hard way. The Barrett M107 weighs 29.98lb empty; a filled magazine can add 2.2lb or so, depending on the number of cartridges loaded. (US DoD)

> The Soldiers on the roof [of the compound] continuously exchanged fire with the enemy. "We had to expend a lot of ammo," Specialist Marvin Speckhaus said. "We didn't see where they were coming from." Some of the scouts worked in teams. On the east wall, Sergeant Ryan Spinelli and Specialist Erik Howes alternated firing M203 rounds while the other reloaded. Later at the compound entrance, Howes directed some ANA Soldiers to return fire. Sergeant Mike Brilla and Specialist Joseph Wilhelm took turns firing an M107 Barrett sniper rifle while the other spotted. Brilla used it to shoot holes in a wall concealing an insurgent gunman. The .50-caliber bullets penetrated the wall but Brilla had no idea if he scored any hits. He later spotted an insurgent holding a radio and alerted Wilhelm, but before Wilhelm could fire, the man disappeared. Even if the insurgent had presented a target, Wilhelm could not have shot him. "If he only has a radio, you can't pop him," said Brilla. The rules of engagement prevented the scouts from firing on anyone without a weapon. "They'll shoot at you," said Brilla, then "they drop their weapons and they just walk away." (Wright 2010: 165)

This account is interesting in that it illustrates both the power and the restraint in the hands of a Barrett operator. The formidable penetration of the rifle is used to deprive the enemy of the value of solid cover, such as the earthen walls lacing the fields nearby. At the same time, the snipers aren't simply pumping away at any targets that present themselves – they stick to the rules of engagement (ROE), which in the intensity of a combat situation indicates an impressive level of willpower. The battle around OP Dusty lasted for two days, and included US air attacks and aerial resupply missions to keep the determined insurgents at bay. Finally the attackers relented and gave up, the snipers and the other US troops having offered heroic and persistent resistance.

Another example of a Barrett engagement illustrates just what a difference a single weapon can make to the outcome of a battle. The location was Lutayfiyah, Iraq, and the date was April 9, 2004. Fourteen US Marines from Fox Company, 2nd Battalion, 2nd Marine Regiment, were tasked with entering and patrolling the area, and were given overwatch by

Marine sniper Staff Sergeant Steve Reichert, awarded the Bronze Star for his handling of a Barrett during the battle of Lutayfiyah, Iraq, on April 9, 2004. (US DoD)

Marine sniper Staff Sergeant Steve Reichert, accompanied by his spotter, positioned on the top of an elevated oil tower some 914m (1,000yd) away from the patrol. Reichert was armed with an M82A3 Special Applications Scoped Rifle. Speaking in a TV documentary (*Sniper: Inside the Crosshairs*, History Channel, 2010), Reichert justified his choice of weapon: "If we had strong winds or anything else, I wanted something that would fight the wind a little bit better; and if insurgents took up covered positions, whether inside a building or behind a car, I wanted something that would actually punch through the material and take them out."

From the overwatch position, the spotter noticed a suspicious dead animal in the middle of one of the roads in the town, and closer inspection through the scopes indicated the presence of an IED under the corpse. The Marine patrol was radioed and informed of the threat, and they took up perimeter positions at a safe distance from it. Before engineers could arrive and get to work, however, the streets suddenly erupted in ripples of small-arms and RPG fire, as insurgents launched an ambush. "Once I saw the firefight start to erupt, I made a quick range estimation [1,275m (1,350yd)], put the correct dope on the scope [adjusted for windage and elevation], and then just started scanning for targets of opportunity." There were plenty to fire at. While the Marines were forced to grab cover in an abandoned schoolhouse, Reichert could see insurgents from all over the town swarming into the area to participate in the firefight, heavily outnumbering the Americans. Reichert now had to even out the odds. The first target he selected was an insurgent popping up on a roof to fire his AK assault rifle at the Marines. The first shot Reichert fired went low, but after correction advice from his spotter he fired again, this time turning his enemy into a "pink mist."

Reichert then noticed three heavily armed insurgents taking up position behind the wall of a stairwell, obscuring them from his view. Reichert marked what he thought was their position behind the wall with his crosshairs, but the range of this position was more than 1,600m (1,750yd) from the oil tower. This was when the Barrett's specialist ammunition came into play, for Reichert was armed with Mk 211 Raufoss cartridges – perfect for a long-range shot at an enemy hiding behind protective cover.

After scope adjustments based on advice from his spotter, Reichert steadied his breathing and squeezed off another round. "The round landed exactly where we wanted it to. The wall on the opposite side of that stairwell just turned red. We didn't see the three of them get up." This was an astonishing shot. There are surely few weapons in the modern panoply of small arms that can kill or incapacitate three enemy combatants, all hidden behind a wall, at a range of more than a mile with a single bullet. Reichert was eventually to spend 12 hours taking down insurgents during the battle, turning the course of the engagement in favor of the US troops. He was awarded the Bronze Star for this action.

The kill totals for Barrett use in Afghanistan and Iraq must now surely be counted in the hundreds, if not the thousands. Few weapons are so trusted in service by US forces, the boom of the Barrett giving reassurance to other troops that someone is watching their backs.

IMPACT
Barrett in the crosshairs

FOREIGN MILITARY USE

So far this book has predominantly focused on the Barrett in the hands of US forces, by far the biggest user of the .50-caliber rifles. But beyond US troops, more than 60 other nations around the world have taken the weapons into their arsenals, and many of them into combat.

The British Army, for example, has adopted the Barrett M82A1 under the designation L82A1, and used it to good effect in both Iraq and Afghanistan. It has found particular favor among the ranks of the Royal Marines and the Special Air Service (SAS). In November 2001, two SAS squadrons (A and G) conducted a major operation to destroy an al-Qaeda opium-storage facility and base near to Afghanistan's southern border

USAF Technical Sergeant Elizabeth Beckley, Special Tactics Training Squadron, explains to Secretary of the Air Force Michael Donley the physical and tactical characteristics of the Barrett M107. (US DoD)

British forces have adopted the Barrett M82A1 as the L82A1. Here a Royal Marine from 40 Commando practices with the rifle from the deck of HMS *Ocean* in the Persian Gulf. (Pa / PA Archive/Press Association Images)

with Pakistan. The audacious action began with a high-altitude low-opening (HALO) parachute jump by eight men of Air Troop, who marked a landing strip to allow six C-130 Hercules aircraft to fly straight into the area and deposit 120-plus men in 36 vehicles. G Squadron then formed a fire support base (FSB) to provide stand-off support, while A Squadron assaulted the enemy base. Many of the G Squadron personnel were armed with the L82A1, and soon al-Qaeda fighters were dropping from the long-range rifle fire, or at least taking cover from it. The Barrett rifles proved

Spanish Marine, Gulf of Aden, 2002 (opposite)

A Spanish marine armed with a Barrett M95, aboard the Santa Maria-class frigate *Navarra* (F85), provides cover for a helicopter-deployed boarding team during a hostile boarding of the North Korean freighter *So San*. With US intelligence having identified that the vessel was transporting ballistic missiles and missile components from North Korea to the Middle East, on December 9, 2002 the US authorities asked the Spanish Navy, which had been tailing the *So San*, to stop, board, and search the vessel as it transited the Gulf of Aden. Two frigates made the interdiction, with one, the *Navarra*, using its main gun to fire three warning shots across the *So San*'s bow to bring the ship to a halt. Then Spanish special forces rappeled onto the deck of the ship from an SH-3 Sea King helicopter, with Barrett-armed snipers providing overwatch. Although a single-shot weapon, the M95 was actually perfect for this role; its ultra-accuracy meant it could lock onto targets in close proximity to the friendly troops landing on the deck. The sniper here also has green-tipped armor-piercing rounds laid ready at his side. As the incident unfolded, thankfully the snipers were not called upon to fire, although the subsequent search of the *So San* bore fruit, revealing that the freighter was carrying 15 complete Scud tactical ballistic missiles, 15 warheads, and barrels of rocket propellant.

Special-operations troops of the Royal Malaysian Air Force receive instruction from a US serviceman in how to handle the M107, 2009. (Technical Sergeant Aaron Cram, USAF)

essential for dominating the enemy, allowing A Squadron more secure avenues of attack and leading to the ultimate success of the mission.

British special forces have also found a new way to increase the portability of the Barrett in a battlefield context. In November 2014, reports began to appear in the British press about SAS operations against Islamic State (IS) insurgents operating inside Iraq. In one tactical innovation, IS personnel would be identified by drone surveillance, then Chinook helicopters would quickly deploy SAS hunter teams to the area. The teams would leave the Chinooks on specially adapted quad bikes, which either mounted L7A1 machine guns or carried .50-caliber Barrett rifles, and would be used to get the SAS men to their firing positions. From there, as they told the newspaper reporters: "We're degrading their morale. They can run and hide if they see planes in the sky but they can't see or hear us. Using so many snipers takes the fear factor to another level too; the terrorists don't know what's happening. They just see their colleagues lying dead in the sand."

Britain is just one of dozens of military Barrett users around the world. They include Argentina, Australia, Belgium, Brazil, Finland, Greece, Italy, Malaysia, Norway, Pakistan, Saudi Arabia, Singapore, Sweden, Tunisia, and Ukraine. To give this list some context, many of the Barretts go to elite forces for specialist sniper duties, rather than as general issue to regular infantry units. Some of the special-forces groups which employ Barrett rifles include Australia's Special Operations Command (M82A1), Malaysia's Grup Gerak Khas (M95), Royal Thai Navy SEALs (M95), Israel's Combat Engineering Corps (M82A1), and Poland's Wojska Specjalne (M107). Barretts are the long-arm firepower of many of the world's best troops.

CONTROVERSY AND CONTROL

Although the Barrett's biggest customers are military, these incredibly powerful weapons are also available for civilian sales in many countries across the world. Even in the UK, that most restrictive environment for acquiring and using firearms, a bolt-action Barrett can be purchased and fired, as long as the buyer has the appropriate firearms license, no criminal record, and can demonstrate that he is acquiring the gun for a specific sporting purpose.

During "Soldiers' Day" in San Salvador, El Salvador, May 7, 2011, a civilian rides past soldiers parading with M107 Barretts; note the different styles of muzzle brakes. (Pa / PA Archive/Press Association Images)

The open availability of Barrett rifles is one of the factors that have made Barrett Firearms Manufacturing, Inc. such a commercial success. Yet it has also brought the Barrett a heavy measure of controversy, as the weapons have often ended up in the hands of those on the darker side of the legal divide.

In the United States, in the late 1990s, there began a groundswell of political animosity against .50-caliber Barrett rifles. Several anti-gun activist bodies, along with a group of supporters in government in Washington, DC, began lobbying for and attempting to legislate against the sale of .50-caliber rifles (but the Barrett in particular), arguing that they were ending up in the hands of national and international terrorists. Domestically, concerns had been raised as early as 1993, when Barrett rifles had been used by the Branch Davidian cult during the ill-fated siege in Waco, Texas, which resulted in the deaths of 76 people (none due to Barrett fire, it should be pointed out). In 2001, the Violence Policy Center (a US-based gun-control organization) published a study entitled *Voting From the Rooftops: How the Gun Industry Armed Osama bin Laden, Other Foreign and Domestic Terrorists, and Common Criminals with 50 Caliber Sniper Rifles*. The article began what has been a bitter running battle between Barrett Firearms Manufacturing, Inc. and the VPC, particularly centered upon the accusation that the al-Qaeda terrorist group had bought 25 Barrett rifles in the United States, then shipped them out to the Middle East where they could be used against Western forces. Ronnie Barrett and his company have vigorously responded to these accusations; and it should be made clear that none of the accusations has ever pointed to a criminal case or a proof of irresponsibility, just a company operating legitimately within the limits of US gun law. The VPC also pointed to what it saw as the proliferation of the .50-caliber rifle in the criminal community, listing and updating numerous examples of Barrett rifles being involved in or connected to criminal activity.

The campaign against the .50-caliber Barretts gathered pace in Congress, with some senators fielding direct policies to restrict the sale of Barrett rifles to civilians. A flavor of the types of legislation advocated is given here, as part of the Fifty-Caliber Sniper Weapon Regulation Act of 2004. The presentation was given by Senator Carl Levin:

> Fifty caliber sniper rifles are sold not only to military buyers, they are also available to private individuals in the United States. Under current law, .50 caliber sniper rifles nearly identical to those described in the Army's report can be purchased by private individuals with only minimal Federal regulation. In fact, these dangerous weapons are treated the same as other long rifles including shotguns, hunting rifles, and smaller target rifles.
>
> I am a cosponsor of the Fifty-Caliber Sniper Weapon Regulation Act introduced by Senator Feinstein, D-CA. This bill would reclassify .50 caliber rifles under the National Firearms Act, NFA, treating them the same as other high powered or especially lethal firearms like machine guns and sawed off shotguns. Among other things, reclassification of .50 caliber sniper rifles under the NFA would subject them to new registration requirements. Future transfers or sales of .50 caliber sniper rifles would have to be conducted through a licensed dealer with an accompanying background check. In addition, the rifle being sold would have to be registered with Federal authorities.
>
> Adoption of the common sense Fifty-Caliber Sniper Weapon Regulation Act would help to ensure that these dangerous weapons are not obtained by terrorists and used against innocent Americans. We can, and must, do more to help keep military style firearms out of the hands of potential terrorists. (US Congress 2005: 15174)

Some legislative movements against the Barrett have taken hold, but only at state level; there are no significant federal restrictions on Barrett sales in the United States. California, the District of Columbia, and Connecticut, however, have largely banned the manufacture, sale, and ownership of .50-caliber rifles (in California and Connecticut, pre-ban weapons are permitted, but in the District of Columbia the ban is absolute), while Maryland allows ownership but with more intense background checks. The Barrett, however, continues to appear in the gun-control lobby's sights. In 2008, police officials and legislators attempted (unsuccessfully)

OPPOSITE A US Army soldier assigned to Alaska's C Troop 1st Squadron (Airborne) demonstrates the shoulder-carry method of transporting the Barrett. (US Army)

The Barrett has appeared in many popular video games; here Uwe Kielmann, publisher of *GameStar* and *GamePro* magazines, poses in Los Angeles with a Barrett alongside two US Army Green Berets. (Pa / PA Archive/Press Association Images)

to have the rifle banned from private ownership on the island of Honolulu – an attempt that produced a focused response from Ronnie Barrett – and similar bills also collapsed in New York in 2015.

So where is the Barrett rifle in the midst of all this controversy? I do not intend to explore all the arguments and counterarguments in depth, as to do so would virtually take a book in its own right. However, it is right to demythologize the Barrett somewhat, for in some ways it is a victim of its own success. Because of its sheer power, Hollywood (and TV) has given the weapon starring roles in major movies including *Predator 2* (1990), *Navy SEALs* (1990), *Mission: Impossible III* (2006), *Battleship* (2012), and *Terminator: Genisys* (2015). This big-screen presentation has given the .50-caliber Barrett rifles something of a bad-boy image, and has doubtless boosted civilian sales.

When we actually look at the impact of the Barrett *outside* military use, however, the picture is both complex and geographically variable. Within the United States, the contribution of the Barrett to actual criminal activity is extremely low indeed. The VPC-compiled list of crime-related incidents that have involved Barrett rifles (http://www.vpc.org/snipercrime. htm) largely relate to Barretts that were discovered as part of a criminal arsenal, rather than actually being used in action (within the United States at least). That said, there are some notable exceptions. On June 4, 2004, one Marvin Heemeyer of Granby, Colorado, unleashed vengeance on his home town with a Komatsu D355-A bulldozer, which he had up-armored with steel plate and concrete. Inside the vehicle was a veritable arsenal: a .223-caliber Ruger Mini-14 rifle, a .308-caliber Fabrique Nationale rifle, a TEC-9 submachine gun, a .357 Magnum revolver – and a .50-caliber Barrett M82A1. Heemeyer managed to destroy or damage 13 buildings with his bulldozer, but the only firearm he discharged was the revolver, into his own mouth, when his vehicle was finally disabled.

A closer study of the VPC list of incidents reveals that overall the Barrett rifle is, in comparative terms, rarely encountered in a criminal context in the United States, with just 47 incidents listed, most of which did not involve the rifles being discharged. Of course, any criminal armed with a Barrett is a situation to be avoided, but taken in context the level of threat posed is extremely low. Consider that over the last 20 years, 70–90 percent of guns used in all crimes in the United States have been handguns, the true weapon of choice for criminals. Rifles account for about 20–30 percent, but the calibers involved in most crimes involving such firearms are the most popular and most accessible, such as .22 rimfire, .223

Remington, and .30-06. We should also bear in mind the very low levels of production of .50-caliber rifles when compared to other species of rifle. A report by the Bureau of Alcohol, Tobacco, Firearms and Explosives (ATF) entitled *Annual Firearms Manufacturing and Export Report* (2013), lists total American firearms production in 2011, broken down by manufacturer. Total production of firearms that year included 2,598,133 handguns, 2,318,088 rifles, 862,401 shotguns, and 190,407 "miscellaneous firearms." Now consider that Barrett Firearms Manufacturing, Inc. produced just 1,866 weapons *of all types* during that year, and that most of those would have certainly gone to military customers. Taken as a proportion of total American firearms output, Barrett production was a tiny fraction of the weapons circulated. (Remington Firearms' production of rifles, for example, was more than 276,000.)

The truth is that Barrett rifles are rarely used in anger in criminal activity within the United States. Putting aside the issues of availability and high cost, Barretts are not straightforward weapons to use tactically when in the hands of people outside the military context. Barretts are heavy, noisy, unwieldy, and comparatively slow to bring to action compared to a light assault rifle or a magazine-fed semiautomatic handgun. Any criminal wanting to retain some freedom of movement in his plans – and that is most of them – will almost always go for light, portable firearms, not hefty weapons like the Barrett.

Note that I am not making an argument either for or against gun control *per se* – this title is not the place for such philosophically and legally voluminous debates. Nor am I denying the possibility that a Barrett might be used in the United States one day to inflict serious loss of life. What I would argue, however, is that taken in the context of the entirety of gun ownership and gun crime in the United States, singling out the Barrett when its contribution to criminality is tiny, and will likely remain so, seems a somewhat misguided focus.

ON BOTH SIDES OF THE LAW

Bearing in mind what has just been said about the limitations of the Barrett, there are unfortunately some international contexts in which terrorist organizations have found a regular and nefarious purpose for the rifle. Because the distribution of the Barrett is virtually global, and to civilian as well as military markets, it is almost inevitable that some will filter through the cracks into the wrong hands. This situation has been most pronounced in Mexico, where the personal armies of the major drugs cartels have found the Barrett useful in the context of the internecine drug wars that have blighted the country and the lives of its people. The violent struggle between law enforcement and the cartels (and between the cartels themselves) is actually on a par with a substantial civil war – since 2006, it is estimated that more than 140,000 people have been killed.

The deep pockets of the drugs cartels have enabled them to acquire plentiful heavy weaponry, including some numbers of Barrett rifles and other .50-caliber varieties. These weapons seem to be used as much for

Mexican Army general Antonio Erasto Monsivais, responsible for decommissioning arms seized in the drugs war, holds up a brand-new Barrett M99, captured during a raid. (Pa / PA Archive/Press Association Images)

their powers of psychological intimidation as for their tactical roles.

In the early-morning hours of February 19, 2013, Gustavo Gerardo Garza Saucedo, the police chief in Nuevo Leon, was murdered by a sniper using a .50-caliber rifle shot when he arrived home in Apodaca, 12.5 miles northwest of the capital. What is shocking about this incident is that the shooting range was estimated to be about 60m (66yd), a range at which a simple assault rifle would be infinitely more practical. The reason for using the .50-caliber would seem to be that of delivering as much physical carnage as possible, and thus projecting a very visible warning to others. Furthermore, and returning to the point made earlier about Barretts being hard to use in a criminal context, apparently a tripod mounting device was left behind at the scene as the criminal fled. This might be an error in journalism – it was more likely the gun's bipod – but whatever the case it suggests a gunman who was not only ill-trained in handling the weapon, but also likely struggling to make his getaway with such an encumbrance.

Barretts and other .50-caliber rifles have been used in several assassinations in the Mexican conflict. They have also been utilized in anti-materiel actions, principally against law-enforcement/military vehicles and helicopters. Some sources list a total of nine recorded incidents involving Barrett rifles in Mexico between January 2008 and February 2013. The incidents include the killing of eight corrections officers in an ambush during a prisoner transfer in Nayarit on April 19, 2009, the officers being struck down in their armored prisoner vehicle while it was moving. In May 2011, a total of five federal helicopters were struck by Barrett shots, on some occasions forcing the helicopters to land and inflicting serious injuries upon their occupants. And these are only the incidents we know about. Barretts and other .50-caliber rifles are doubtless being unleashed in the context of the endless inter-cartel battles well away from media view. The Barretts are not only fired in the conventional shoulder-mounted manner, but on occasions have been adapted for improvised vehicular mounts set in the back of standard station wagon (estate) vehicles. One photograph shows the rear seats of such a vehicle having been removed, and the Barrett attached to what appears to be a crude pintle mount. To fire the gun, the vehicle's trunk door was swung up and open, the shooter operating the gun

The Barrett M90 rifle used in the murder of Lance Bombardier Stephen Restorick at Bessbrook in Northern Ireland on February 12, 1997. The presence of the Barretts in the province was a threat for a period of seven years. (Pa / PA Archive/Press Association Images)

from near the backs of the front seats. Given that the muzzle brake appears to be venting back into the interior of the car, the blast and report of the Barrett on firing must have been immense.

So in Mexico, the Barrett rifle does indeed seem to be something of a problem. Yet once again, some context is needed. For a start, care must be taken to avoid using the word "Barrett" as shorthand for any .50-caliber rifle. As the conclusion to this book will explain, the Barretts are far from the only .50 BMG weapons now on the market; they just have the most identifiable brand name. Also, it must be remembered that the drugs cartels are not groups of low-level criminals, but structured (albeit violent) organizations supported by literally millions of narco-dollars. A handful of Barretts is just a fraction of the criminal arsenal, which according to security experts now includes .30- and .50-caliber Browning machine guns, fragmentation grenades, landmines, mortars, rocket-propelled grenades, and even, some sources claim, shoulder-launched anti-aircraft missiles. Again, singling out the Barrett rifle in such a context seems rather selective, although obviously it is in everyone's interests to cut off the flow of such weapons to illegal organizations.

Mexico is far from the only country in which the Barrett has appeared to acquire local notoriety. In Britain, Barretts came to public attention most graphically during the operations of the "South Armagh Sniper" in Northern Ireland in 1990–97, a terrible episode worthy of a little deeper exploration. During this period, multiple snipers (not just one, as the title suggests) within the Provisional Irish Republican Army (IRA) conducted a ruthlessly pursued sniping campaign against British Army soldiers and Northern Irish security personnel in the beautiful but troubled county of Armagh, in the south-eastern corner of the province. Seven British Army soldiers and two Royal Ulster Constabulary (RUC) constables were killed and one constable wounded – significant losses made all the more traumatic for the British by the fact that all but three of the victims were killed by heavy .50-caliber fire from Barrett rifles. The IRA's acquisition of these rifles meant that they could make the shots from distant stand-off range, often near the border with the Irish Republic, across which they could make a rapid escape. British anti-sniper operations by special forces resulted in the capture of some of the IRA snipers and their .50-caliber weapons in 1997, while the Good Friday agreement concluded the entire campaign. It is worth noting that the last British soldier to die in Northern Ireland, Lance Bombardier Stephen Restorick, was killed by a .50-caliber Barrett sniper bullet.

The .50-caliber rifles used by the IRA during the campaign were the M82 and the M90. Unlike many of the IRA's weapons, which were frequently imported from Libya and Eastern Europe, the Barretts came from the United States, purchased by American IRA sympathizers and smuggled into the Irish Republic, then across the border into Northern Ireland, either whole or in parts for later reassembly. Around these weapons, the IRA created coherent sniper teams of 4–20 personnel, the shooter being supported by a varying number of spotters and reconnaissance operators. South Armagh is a compact and undulating landscape bisected by walls, woods, hedgerows, and orchards, so the range of the shots was always well within the Barrett's efficiency – typically the shots were taken at about 300m (328yd). Sometimes the firing position was in the open, but the IRA also adapted a Mazda 626 as a sniper vehicle, creating a firing position around the back seats and applying improvised armor to protect the occupants from return fire.

The presence of Barrett rifles, as with so many other types of weapons, brought tragedy to the roads and lanes of Northern Ireland. They also spread fear among British troops and security forces, all of whom were grimly aware that their body armor was impotent against such rounds.

To this day, Barretts continue to reside in terrorist arsenals, and are sometimes a focal point of major engagements. Outside of the major military engagements in Iraq and Afghanistan, and the clashes in Mexico and other troubled Latin American states, the Philippines has seen some of the most intensive Barrett action. On January 25, 2015, for example, the Special Action Force (SAF) of the Philippine National Police (PNP) conducted a major operation against the Bangsamoro Islamic Freedom Fighters (BIFF) and the Moro Islamic Liberation Front (MILF) at Tukanalipao, Mamasapano, and Maguindanao in the Philippines. The action deteriorated into a brutal and particularly bloody gun battle in which the rebels utilized, to punishing effect, significant numbers of Barretts and other .50-caliber rifles. Heavily outgunned, the SAF took 44 killed. Rodolfo "Boogie" Mendoza, Jr., president of the Philippine Institute for Peace Terrorism Violence Research (PIPVTR), later told a reporter concerning the dead: "Their faces were blown apart, their limbs were shattered, that's the mark of a Barrett Caliber .50, the weapon of choice of MILF-BIFF snipers" (quoted in Politiko 2015).

While it is possible to list other incidents such as these, to do so runs the risk of presenting the Barrett rifle as an underworld weapon, which taken in terms of its total distribution it most certainly is not, for Barretts have also been acquired globally in large numbers not only by counterterrorist forces, but also by numerous police forces looking to add an anti-materiel element to their arsenals.

CONCLUSION

When the Barrett rifle first appeared during the 1980s, it was something of a revelation. The destructive power, the reach, the sensation of firing – here was a weapon in another league, and one that offered a genuinely portable anti-materiel and ultra-long-range sniping capability. Once it started selling well to military forces, law-enforcement agencies, and civilians, the rest of the world's gunmakers sat up and took note.

Today, the Barrett rifle takes its place among a prolific arsenal of .50-caliber AMRs and sniper rifles. (Note that there are now many AMRs manufactured in calibers other than .50-caliber, such as the 14.5×114mm Russian, 12.7×108mm, and various 20mm calibers.) Some of these rifles have become genuine rivals to the Barrett on the international market.

Range work is the foundation of a good Barrett shot, as it enables the shooter to build up experience and data across the full spectrum of ranges. These men are alternating between an M107 and the M110 Semi Automatic Sniper System. (US DoD)

Seen through grainy night-vision goggles, Canadian snipers fire a McMillan TAC-50 SASR during a night exercise with US Marines at Camp Pendleton, California, 2013. (USMC)

Chief among these is the McMillan TAC-50, a .50 BMG bolt-action rifle which emerged in the late 1980s and now has an established and widespread customer base that includes the Canadian Army (as the C15 Long Range Sniper Weapon), Israeli Special Forces, the South African Police Service Special Task Force, and also the US Navy SEALs. French company PGM Précision makes a popular .50 BMG rifle, the Hécate II; and Eastern European countries have also invested much effort into the type, notable systems including the Hungarian Gepárd (available in 12.7×108mm, .50 BMG, and 14.5×114mm), the 14.5mm Istiglal of Azerbaijan, and the 12.7×108mm KSVK of Russia.

Britain entered the market in earnest in the 2000s, with Accuracy International producing three 12.7×99mm weapons: the bolt-action, magazine-fed AW50 (with a folding-stock version, the AW50F) and the related AX50, and the gas-operated semiautomatic AS50. The Steyr company of Austria produces two AMRs: the .50 BMG single-shot bolt-action HS .50 (also available in .460 Steyr) and the innovative IWS (Infantry Weapon System) 2000, which fires a 15.2×169mm armor-piercing fin-stabilized discarding-sabot round from a smoothbore barrel. Add in numerous other AMRs manufactured around the world, and it can be seen that Barrett is no longer alone in its field.

Nevertheless, Barrett Firearms Manufacturing, Inc. still stands out from the crowd, due in part to the prominent market position the company has forged for itself – it is commercially efficient, and maximizes its brand profile. The company is also an innovative by nature, releasing new products and accessories to keep up with market trends. Yet the main reason for its occupation of the high ground is, ultimately, the quality of its products. Barrett rifles have been through more than two decades of extreme combat testing, and have not been found wanting. They perfectly fulfill the role for which they were designed – long-range destructive sniper fire – and they have proven that they can cope with all the hard knocks of military life and extreme environments. Like the M2HB machine gun and the AK-47 assault rifle, Barrett rifles such as the M82A1/M107 are likely to be the type of weapons that remain in use for decades, not years, to come.

BIBLIOGRAPHY

Alaimo, Mark (2011). *Duty. Honor. My Country*. Bloomington, IN: Xlibris.

Barrett (2011). *M107A1 Operator's Manual*. Murfreesboro, TN: Barrett Firearms Manufacturing, Inc.

Barrett (n.d.). *Operator's Manual: .50 Caliber Rifle M82A1*. Murfreesboro, TN: Barrett Firearms Manufacturing, Inc.

Barrett (n.d.). *Operator's Manual: M107A1*. Murfreesboro, TN: Barrett Firearms Manufacturing, Inc.

Barrett (n.d.). *Operator's Manual: Model 98B*. Murfreesboro, TN: Barrett Firearms Manufacturing, Inc.

Barrett (n.d.). *Operator's Manual: MRAD (Multi-Role Adaptive Design)*. Murfreesboro, TN: Barrett Firearms Manufacturing, Inc.

Barrett Firearms Manufacturing, Inc. website: **https://www.barrett.net/**

Barrett, Ronnie (2008). "A tour of Barrett Firearms, Part 2." Transcript of YouTube video interview, uploaded July 1, 2008: **https://www.youtube.com/watch?v=kLBmc-Lgtb0**

Barrett, Ronnie (March 14, 2008). *Letter to Chief Boisse Correa of the Honolulu Police Department from Ronnie Barrett*.

Bureau of Alcohol, Tobacco, Firearms and Explosives (2013). *Annual Firearms Manufacturing and Export Report 2011*. Martinsburg, WV: ATF.

Haskew, Michael E. (2012). *The Sniper at War: From the American Revolutionary War to the Present Day*. London: Amber Books.

Jane's International Defence Review (June 1, 1994). "A tale of two fifties; 0.50-calibre sniper rifles gain popularity."

Lamothe, Dan (2012). "Snipers seek better weapons, ammo." *The Marine Corps Times*, November 20, 2012. Available online at: **http://archive.marinecorpstimes.com/article/20121120/ NEWS/211200322/Snipers-seek-better-weapons-ammo**

Lewis, Jack (2011). *The Gun Digest Book of Assault Weapons*. Iola, WI: Krause Publishing.

Pegler, Martin (2006). *Out of Nowhere: A history of the military sniper, from the sharpshooter to Afghanistan*. Oxford: Osprey Publishing.

Pegler, Martin (2007). *Sniper: A History of the US Marksman*. Oxford: Osprey Publishing.

Plaster, John (2006). *The Ultimate Sniper: An advanced training manual for military and police snipers (Updated and Expanded)*. Boulder, CO; Paladin Press.

Plaster, John (2008). *The History of Sniping and Sharpshooting*. Boulder, CO: Paladin Press.

Plaster, John (2012). "The Barrett .50 Caliber." NRA American Rifleman website. Available online at: **http://www.americanrifleman.org/articles/2012/12/13/the-barrett-50-caliber/**

Politiko.com (2015). "Barrett .50Cal: Muslim sniper's weapon of choice in Mamasapano massacre." Available online at: **http://politics.com.ph/barrett-50cal-muslim-snipers-weapon-of-choice-in-mamasapano-massacre/**

Smith, Jim (2003). *Operation Iraqi Freedom: PEO Soldier Lessons Learned*. Available online at: **http://www.militec-1.com/OperationIraqiFreedom.pdf**

Snow, Kimberley (2007). "Brigade Reconnaissance Troop plays major role in Fallujah offensive." US 1st Infantry News website. Available online at: **http://www.riley.army.mil/News/ArticleDisplay/ tabid/98/Article/469655/brigade-reconnaissance-troop-plays-major-role-in-fallujah-offensive.aspx**

US Army (1994). FM 23-10 *Sniper Training*. Washington, DC: Department of the Army.

US Army (2003). FM 3-05.222 *Special Forces Sniper Training*. Washington, DC: Department of the Army.

US Army (2014). *Operator's Manual: Long Range Sniper Rifle (LRSR), Caliber .50, M107* (Nsn 1005-01-469-2133). Washington, DC: Department of the Army.

US Marine Corps (1981). FMFM 1-3B *Sniping*. Washington, DC: Headquarters of the Navy.

Violence Policy Center (2001). *Voting From the Rooftops: How the Gun Industry Armed Osama bin Laden, Other Foreign and Domestic Terrorists, and Common Criminals with 50 Caliber Sniper Rifles*. Washington, DC: Violence Policy Center. Available online at: **http://www.vpc.org/studies/ roofcont.htm**

Wright, Donald P., ed. (2010). *Vanguard of Valor: Small-unit actions in Afghanistan*. Fort Leavenworth, KS: US Army Combined Arms Center.

INDEX